EDUCATING THE INNOVATIVE
PUBLIC MANAGER

Educating the Innovative Public Manager

Samuel I. Doctors

*Graduate School of Business
University of Pittsburgh*

W. Henry Lambright

*The Maxwell School
Syracuse University*

Donald C. Stone

*School of Urban and Public Affairs
Carnegie-Mellon University*

with the assistance of
Jo Ann M. Eliason

  Oelgeschlager, Gunn & Hain, Publishers, Inc.
Cambridge, Massachusetts

International Standard Book Number: 0-89946-079-8

Library of Congress Catalog Card Number: 80-39481

Printed in West Germany

Library of Congress Cataloging in Publication Data

Doctors, Samuel I
   Educating the innovative public manager.

   Includes index.
   1. Public administration—Study and teaching—United States   2. Government executives, Training of—United States.   3. Technological innovations—United States. I. Lambright, W. Henry, 1939– joint author. II. Stone, Donald Crawford, 1903– joint author.
III. Title.
JF1338.A2D59   350'.0007'073   80-39481

ISBN 0-89946-079-8

Any opinions, findings, and conclusions or recommendations expressed in this publication are those of the authors and do not necessarily reflect the views of the National Science Foundation.

Contents

List of Tables

Foreword

Since the late 1960s, the Intergovernmental Programs of the National Science Foundation has been working in partnership with other federal agencies, state and local governments, universities, federal laboratories, and other research institutions. The goal of this partnership arrangement has been to explore and develop improved institutional capabilities and systems for heightening the contribution of the nation's considerable scientific and technological resources to the resolution of domestic sector issues and problems.

This endeavor has resulted in the development of a considerable body of dedicated individuals in both user and research-performing institutions across the country who are committed to improving the quality of American life through a more effective and efficient use of science and technology in the public sector. It has also resulted in the establishment, testing, and, in many cases, the institutionalization of increased technological capacity in our state and local governments. Innovative processes and structures for combining the knowledge users and the producers have been developed, and much has been learned from systematic research about the conditions and methods for achieving innovation in the public sector.

During the period in which this public technology activity has taken place, we have developed considerable understanding about institutional capacity, linkages, and the process of innovation itself. Looking to the future, several questions have arisen: Can this knowledge be packaged in such a way so as to make a contribution to the education of persons entering, or working in, the field of public administration and related areas? How can this be done? What are the potentials for good that could be realized from such a venture?

It was with such questions in mind that the National Science Foundation Intergovernmental Programs contacted three nationally recognized experts to address themselves to these questions from their perspectives. Their task has been to assess needs and potential, to define initiatives that would contribute most in tangible benefits, and to indicate mechanics and resource requirements.

The chapters in this volume constitute the papers of the experts: Samuel I. Doctors, Professor of Business Administration, Graduate School of Business, University of Pittsburgh, and Director of the Energy Policy Institute at the university; W. Henry Lambright, Professor of Political Science and Public Administration, The Maxwell School, Syracuse University, and Director of the Science and Technology Policy Center, Syracuse Research Corporation; and Donald C. Stone, Adjunct Professor of Public Administration, School of Urban and Public Affairs, Carnegie-Mellon University, and Dean Emeritus, Graduate School of Public and International Affairs, University of Pittsburgh. The book also includes a synthesis document prepared by Dr. Lambright highlighting the significant findings, complementary objectives, and varied program initiatives proposed by the authors.

It is hoped that these illuminating chapters and the approaches contained therein will heighten the sense of real importance and urgency attached to this issue. Further, it is hoped that they will serve as the basis for government and foundation support for pilot activities in university settings across the country. If the potential for benefits is as great as the experts project, the inititation of action programs to implement their proposals should lead to a significant strengthening of innovative and other essential administrative capabilities of future executives and managers at all levels of the federal system. Such an effort could well lead to a much-needed increase in the number of managers who understand the necessity, process, and means for implementing the innovations indispensable in improving governmental effectiveness. The papers reflect high potential for broad benefit to Americans in all walks of life from increased attention to the promotion and implementation of innovative approaches in the public sector.

It is hoped that both practitioners and educators will be motivated by the ideas set forth by Professors Doctors, Lambright, and Stone to invest the time, talent, and money needed to develop this area further. In view of the all-pervasive impact of government in a society as complex as ours, who would say that we should not invest as much in the

enrichment of our nation's educational curriculum in public management as we have in such areas as science, medicine, health, and
agriculture?

Robert C. Crawford
Assistant Associate Director
Office of Applications
Mitigation and Research
Federal Emergency Management Agency
(formerly Director, Intergovernmental
Programs, National Science
Foundation)

Acknowledgments

We would like to offer our thanks to three people connected with the Intergovernmental Programs of the National Science Foundation whose encouragement and assistance made possible the papers presented in this book. First of all, we would like to thank Dr. M. Frank Hersman, presently with the Office of Counsel at NSF, who was one of the founders of the Intergovernmental Programs and whose foresightedness helped bring about the accomplishments of these programs and led to the project that culminated in the production of these papers. Second, we owe a debt of gratitude to Mr. Robert C. Crawford, who, as Director of the Intergovernmental Programs, initiated the project and later, in his capacity at the Federal Emergency Management Agency, continued to express his interest in our progress and provide us with valuable advice. Third, we would like to express our great appreciation to Mr. David Richtmann, who, as our project supervisor, provided us with continual encouragement and useful and creative criticism. We thank him for his enthusiasm and assistance throughout this project.

We would also like to thank Ms. Annunciata Marino and Ms. Toni Trofnoff for their assistance in typing the final draft of our manuscript.

This book is sponsored by the Energy Policy Institute of the University of Pittsburgh, which provided us with its resources for our editorial and typing needs.

Chapter 1

Introduction: Toward Curricula for Public Management of Innovation

W. Henry Lambright

In the three chapters that follow, Drs. Stone, Doctors, and I discuss the need for developing university curricula for the public management of innovation. Such curricula would deal with the process of identifying, introducing, and institutionalizing science- and technology-based innovations in the public sector. They would also have the broader aim of teaching skills that can help make managers more innovative in general.

Doctors and I tend to be more concerned with increasing the understanding of science, technology, and innovation as a specific subject focus. Stone is more interested in producing innovative public managers in general and in sectoral or programmatic fields who are capable of developing innovative organizations and applying new technologies.

Our approaches are complementary. We concur on the nature of the problem and major elements of the solution. We offer different components for a common objective. We suggest specific steps that might be taken to address a need that Warren Bennis has called one of the most profound of all: ". . .No. 3 in terms of the key problems which can bring about the destruction of society is the quality of the management and leadership of our institutions. . . .In effect, here we are: virtually without leaders."[1]

THE NATURE OF THE PROBLEM

Public managers are increasingly called upon to cope with both the processes and impacts of change, particularly technological change. Energy, environmental pollution, human service needs, urban development and productivity, governmental regulation, responsibilities to the less developed nations—these and other problems abound. All require innovative responses by public managers. All have large components that involve science and technology. All reveal gaps between what is needed and what is done.

Evidence suggests present managers are not keeping up with the requirements of dealing with change. It is obvious that many who now occupy top- and middle-level positions in the federal-state-local system are in over their heads in relation to present and emerging public problems. Yet their skills and resourcefulness largely determine the ability of organizations to fulfill their purposes effectively and efficiently.

The need for competent managers capable of dealing with change is great at all levels of government. The federal government has long experience in producing change through expenditures for science and technology but much less experience in managing its impacts. Indeed, much of this experience is in limited areas, such as defense and space, where government is both the sponsor and consumer; and it has only been recently that the government has had to deal in a concerted way with other organizations that are consumers of technologies the federal government has funded. Because innovation requires technology transfers from one organization to others, federal officials must be innovative not only by themselves; but they must also seek to help the private sector and state and local government to become more innovative.

For their part, business and state and local officials must constantly adjust to an ever more complex technological society in which interdependencies are the rule rather than the exception. They must deal with issues of cut-back management and meeting new regulations. There is no room for static, bureaucratically sluggish organizations at any level. This is especially the case in those areas concerned with the production and use of scientific and technological knowledge where the need to manage change is most pronounced and where the absence of innovative leadership can have some of its most serious consequences.

We are in agreement that there is a serious problem in public management and that curricula stressing the management of innovation are a useful way to move toward at least some measure of improvement. Performance in the practice of public administration cannot be divorced from the manner in which public managers are prepared (or ill-prepared) by universities.

THE UNIVERSITY RESPONSE

Universities have, for many years, recognized their theoretical obligation to train public managers in order for our democracy to prosper. In practice, they have done little to meet this obligation and have relied on the versatility of those trained in disciplinary specialties to achieve on-the-job managerial expertise. There is a responsibility on the part of the university for public management education that cannot be shirked. University leaders must consider the attributes of successful practitioners and find ways to help those students with the requisite raw ability and desire to emulate such models. Stone notes three desirable kinds of special knowledge and competence in first-rate public managers:[2]

a. Professional competence in handling the tasks, processes, and relationships inherent in the executive/managerial function, that is, in providing organizational leadership, direction, innovation, and effectiveness.

b. Intellectual, entrepreneurial, behavioral, interpersonal and related abilities, traits, motives, maturity, and other characteristics of successful executive managers.

c. Substantive, technological, policy, operational, environmental, and other contextual knowledge and abilities in the fields or jurisdictions in which the managerial or executive role is carried out.

Few universities have designed programs or clusters of courses to develop and strengthen these three categories of traits in any systematic fashion. Fewer, still, have given attention to training for public managers that would strengthen their capabilities for using the advantages of science and technology in solving problems. The performance gap between what is needed in society and what federal, state, and local managers do is mirrored (and is, in part, a consequence of) performance gaps in the university.

Universities, therefore, must look to newer and better ways to train both preentry and inservice students. We agree that there is likely to be continued growth in the public sector, particularly at the state and local levels. The requirements at these levels for overcoming present deficiencies and producing people capable of using new processes and products to solve problems will increase. Recent events at Three Mile Island and at Love Canal attest to this fact. Science and technology have intergovernmental impact, yet how many state and local governments are equipped to deal with the myriad issues of nuclear power, toxic wastes, mass transit, housing, health, and so on?

The federal government seems aware of its need for competent administrative personnel and is providing more and more training opportunities, thanks in part to Office of Personnel Management policies and Senior Executive Service reform. Moreover, a substantial increase in state and local government management training has been fostered with Intergovernmental Personnel Act funds. Society in its needs and government in its demands are stimulating an ever-greater desire for qualified public managers.

Still, the fact is that there is a long way to go in terms of quality of programs provided. Many of the teaching and training programs that are offered are superficial and far from constituting curricula capable of producing managers who can deal with the introduction of innovations, address issues of a scientific or technological nature, are innovative in running their own organization, or are capable of seeking change in and through other organizations.

While there are thus many training and educational activities under way, both preentry and inservice, there is a discontinuity between what is needed and what is supplied. The authors of these chapters see plenty of teaching occurring in public administration (whether in universities or government training centers). Public management courses tend to have good enrollments. Missing are the elements in curricula and faculty commitment intended to increase the innovativeness of managers and trained managers capable of using science, technology, and innovations. This is true in relation to our domestic society as well as the less developed world abroad.

INNOVATION CURRICULA

The authors hold that what are needed are new courses and specializations as a part of curricula designed to meet the administrative needs of the public service and improve the public management of innovation. This entails a set of courses (at least two, preferably more) that will serve to catalyze attention within university and government educational centers to issues concerned with the process of using science- and technology-based innovations in public agencies.

Some teaching material is available that can be reworked for these specific courses. However, the major problem is to establish courses in the first place and to develop instructional packages for those areas where these courses are most needed. Among the major needs we identify are those that deal with executive leadership and policy management as related to innovation and change; those that examine the interface of science and technology with federal, state, and local governments; and those that deal with industry's relation to innovation in the public sector.

Instructional packages geared to public management of innovation would be a valuable addition to any university or inservice training effort. Beyond the specific courses proposed, we hope that such curricula would catalyze broader changes throughout a university's public administration program, not only in substance but also in means of instruction.

In these chapters, there are differences in emphasis and method. Stone gives as much attention to inservice students as to those at a preservice stage. He points to the need for teaching materials that would interest those with strong backgrounds of experience in government. He favors use of "proactive and interactive media" and clinical exercises or projects, and cautions against overly long case studies. Visual aids can play an important role also, he notes.

Doctors takes a somewhat different tack, looking more at preentry public management education at the graduate level. He also gives attention to the role of business schools in public management training. "From my experience in teaching private sector managers," says Doctors, "it appears that graduate schools of business do very little to sensitize their students to the public sector market in general, and even less with regard to the public sector market for new technology. Thus, any suggestions for curriculum designed to train public sector managers to deal more effectively with the evaluation, purchase, and implementation of new technology must also consider the training needs of potential private sector managers who will be the principal means by which technology is sold to the public sector."[3]

The emphasis in my report is on the importance of sensitizing managers to the fact that implementing an innovation, whether scientific, technological, or otherwise, is a political process. It is one that can last a long time, require considerable coalition building, and entail advocacy at every stage. Public managers must do more than analyze and evaluate policies and programs. To implement them, they must sell them to administrative superiors and others whose cooperation is essential. Lawyers have their moot court as part of their training. Public administration students require skill training in advocacy as well, since much of what public managers do involves persuasion in a political environment.

Doctors and I converge around the notion of marketing. Doctors sees the marketing role of the private sector as a key function. I see marketing by the bureaucratic entrepreneur as equally important. Entrepreneurship is a skill that can be honed, strengthened, and improved. Bureaucratic entrepreneurs are aware of public needs and make themselves aware of new technologies and techniques that are available from business. They match what is needed with what is available. Then they move the innovation through the political system.

Stone concentrates on executives and managers as entrepreneurs who need to involve subordinates in developing innovative, productive organizations. He advocates that training in the public management of innovation should be an integral part of the curricula in public management rather than the topic of a few separate courses. He carefully distinguishes public from private executives. Stone is critical of the growth of public sector training in business schools. He quotes Graham Allison, Dean of Harvard's Kennedy School of Government, "that public and private management are at least as different as they are similar, and that the differences are more important than the similarities."[4] Clearly, Stone says, instructional materials used for educating public executives must differ greatly from those applicable to the private sector. Likewise, he declares schools of business are not suitable for programs having a general purpose of preparing public executives and managers.

None of the authors are sanguine about the ease of producing better managers through formal training. All lament existing inadequacies in public administration (and, in Doctors' case, business administration) education. Stone, in particular, criticizes the imbalance between the teaching of academic model building and the actual management skills necessary for public work. He says that most instructors in schools of public affairs/administration/public policy have their Ph.D.s in academic disciplines. This means that they are largely interested in the substance and analytical methods of their discipline. Since they lack a professional/practitioner focus, Stone charges, most have little knowledge of or interest in management, even though it is the central ingredient of public administration and of public policy development and implementation.

DEVELOPING COURSE PACKAGES

The authors call for development of curricula materials to serve the need. Doctors and I emphasize the preparation and adaptation of decision-oriented case studies for public innovation curricula. Stone emphasizes materials for specific teaching units—clinically based instructional packages—having a variety of dimensions. The central idea cutting across the views of all of us is that such materials need to be relevant, lively, and well written. Most importantly, they require dedicated teachers, interested in practitioner competencies, who are capable of making the best use of these materials. Cases, in particular, are only as good as those who use them for class interaction.

The writers present alternative ways of proceeding, depending upon the program's budget. A minimal effort might include building on work now taking place at one or a few institutions, enabling some modest materials to be developed or adapted and then shared. Larger scale efforts could, of course, accomplish much more. Doctors discusses three options, the last of which not only broadens the concept, but also introduces a research component. His most extensive option would cost a university well over $100 thousand.

The gradations of what could be done, discussed by Stone and myself, are not dissimilar to those of Doctors. Stone emphasizes the need to design a "generic" course package focused on executive leadership and the function of management. This is the first of several prepared course packages, and could include units of the management of innovation. Costs would vary with the extensiveness of the package, the amount of time required to produce it, and the nature and extent of its use.

My option would build the public innovation curricula concept from an initial three university base. This consortium of universities would develop and test prototype curricula materials. Such a consortium could hire a writer and/or editor who would work for all three, although one university might play a lead role in terms of managing the actual production of materials.

The authors diverge in emphasis, not in basic thrust of argument, with Doctors and myself being more science and technology oriented and Stone more general management oriented. All are interested in innovation as process and substance. All feel course designs and materials should be tested carefully in a limited number of sites before being widely disseminated. All agree there is a need.

Whether the demand is sufficient to mean that active marketing of the programs will not be required remains to be seen. Views differ among the three of us on the point of marketing and its requirements. On the basis of his experience with similar ventures and a survey of university and government centers, Stone believes that a substantial market exists for the kinds of packages he proposes. He thinks 500 packages of the generic course could be sold. Doctors and I feel a more active marketing effort may be required to move from the early adopters of our materials to a wider group of users.

CONCLUSION

The initial testing of the course packages related to a public management of innovation concept will yield early reactions on the demand for such training. If, as we expect, it meets with a positive response from students and teachers, it would then be adapted to the needs of very different kinds of students and institutions. The ultimate test would lie with what happens to the students, whether preentry or inservice. Our expectation is that they would become more aggressive at seeking out and initiating science and technology based innovations; they would take the time to become aware of the innovations that can help them do their jobs better; they would actively seek out novel approaches to intractable problems. In short, they would be far more likely to succeed in managing change and in becoming masters rather than victims of science and technology.

The quality of our lives depends, in large part, on the talent and skills of those who provide administrative leadership. It is essential that those in key positions of responsibility be prepared to resolve problems. Otherwise, future difficulties will overwhelm them—and us. The preparation of public managers is all-important and universities have a key role in this. The authors of the following chapters are especially concerned that the universities are not fulfilling their role. A more innovative approach to the education of such individuals— particularly in scientific and technological matters—on the part of the universities is needed immediately.

The authors recommend, therefore, that the National Science Foundation, as well as private foundations, provide support to those professors and universities that are willing to move beyond the narrow confines of existing practice. These risk-takers are also the potential pacesetters in public management of innovation education. They should be enabled to develop course materials that could then be diffused to other institutions. This process of diffusion might be enhanced and accelerated via national professional associations in public administration, such as the American Society for Public Administration, the National Association of Schools for Public Affairs and Administration, and the American Public Works Association. Such organizations could serve as vehicles for legitimation and communication. A relatively small investment of funds could thus yield exceptional dividends for the public interest.

NOTES

1. Warren Bennis, *The Unconscious Conspiracy: Why Leaders Can't Lead* (New York: AMACOM, 1976), p. 145.
2. See Chapter 2, p. 15.
3. See Chapter 4, p. 89.
4. Graham T. Allison, Jr., *Public and Private Management: Are They Fundamentally Alike in All Unimportant Aspects?* Discussion Paper Series (Cambridge, Mass.: John Fitzgerald Kennedy School of Government, Harvard University, February 1980).

Education of More Capable and Innovative Public Executives and Managers

Donald C. Stone

Introduction

This chapter seeks to answer several questions:

What is the need for and how important is it to produce more effective, innovative public executives and managers?

What do managers do? What do they need to know?

Are there generic traits, motives, behavior, competencies, and skills which characterize successful executives/managers that can be strengthened by specially designed education and training?

To what extent do universities, governments, and other organizations engage in professional programs focused on developing such knowledge and competencies?

Do present programs meet qualitative and quantitative requirements of local, state, and federal governments?

Is it feasible to develop and package instructional materials to produce more innovative and effective managers and organizations, and how much demand would there be?

How much would it cost to produce an initial demonstration package, what would it cover, and how long would it take?

In seeking answers to these questions, I have engaged in extensive interviewing and correspondence. Numerous books, articles, studies, and reports were examined. Visits were made to a dozen education and training institutions. Contacts have covered government officials, directors of management development and training centers, deans and professors of graduate schools, and professional and public interest groups.

I have drawn heavily on my knowledge of such efforts derived from a recent worldwide assessment conducted for the International Institute of Administrative Sciences and my continuing role as chairman of the International Association of Schools and Institutes of Administration. Experience in designing public administration curricula for a number of universities and organizing and teaching executive management courses has contributed ideas. My wife, Alice, has helped greatly in the conduct of the study.

CONCLUSIONS AND RECOMMENDATIONS

The consultations, correspondence, and research of materials for this project point to three major conclusions: First, the United States requires far more innovative and effective government organizations, executives, and managers to cope with the critical problems and conditions that lie ahead.

Warren Bennis, speaking of a list of the ten most important threats to society, states that after (1) nuclear war or accident, and (2) worldwide epidemic or famine, "No. 3 in terms of the key problems which can bring about the destruction of society is the quality of the management and leadership of our institutions. . . . In effect, here we are: virtually without leaders."[1]

Second, universities and government education/training programs need to strengthen their curricula, courses, and instructional methods. Many need major overhauling. Management-focused curricula and practitioner-oriented instructors are both indispensable in developing the knowledge and competencies required for effective and innovative executive leadership and management of government at all levels.

Third, it is feasible and urgently desirable to prepare operationally intensive course packages. These would be in much demand by universities and training centers.

Role of Management and Innovation

The quality of executives and managers largely determines the capability of organizations to fulfill their purposes effectively and efficiently. Many local, state, and federal agencies perform poorly because of managerial shortcomings. Universities might well be included in this assessment, as few are renowned for innovation and excellence in managing their affairs.

Innovation in government is the conception (through invention, transfer, or adaptation), adoption, and implementation of new objectives, policies, services, ideas, structures, processes, technology, methods, or behavior. Especially sophisticated executives are required to create an innovative and productive organization. They are challenged with modifying or eliminating traditional organizational rigidities. Paralyzing factors include authoritarian hierarchy, inflexible commitment of resources, suppression of conflict, centralized decision making, and rewards for conformity.

Public executives must be especially resourceful and persistent in coping with such obstacles as unresponsive legislative bodies, political chicanery and patronage, power of special and single interest groups, antagonistic media, and citizen apathy. Hence change in the behavior of other actors in the system as well as strengthening of executive competence is usually essential. One official commenting on this project wrote, "If we have learned anything about organizational change, we know that we have to change both the individual and the system, not just the individual." This usually requires legislative action or consent. However, systemic changes often do not take place unless executives point the way and carry through. Many internal malpractices can be curtailed without fundamental changes in the system.

Preentry and Postentry Development

Obviously the preparation of more highly qualified executives/managers to staff city, county, state, and national agencies and enterprises would improve performance. For this purpose two complementary initiatives are essential. The first is to increase substantially the extent and relevance of preentry graduate professional education which provides superior students with managerial knowledge, competence, behavior, motivation, and values of public responsibility. The second way for us to produce superior persons is through inservice executive and management development of various kinds.

Terminology

The author views the terms "executive" and "manager" to be overlapping and somewhat interchangeable, recognizing, however, that the label executive usually refers to top administrative officials. A person in any post which is dominantly managerial in character is appropriately called a manager. The word "supervisor" is used for positions which call for little management of a complex character.

With the establishment of the Senior Executive Service, the U.S. Office of Personnel Mangement (OPM) now refers to "executive development" as the means of increasing leadership and managerial competence of persons in the super-grades. "Management development" is related to senior- and middle-grade levels. Supervisory training picks up at lower levels of responsibility.

The terms "education" and "training" are often alleged to have very distinct meanings. Some view the development of skill or competence to be a matter for training, and not true education. That notion is not very useful. The kind of education dealt with here is professional rather than disciplinary in character, and thus concerned with competence and skills. Suffice it to say that an appropriately educated executive or manager should be a well-trained person.

No significant difference is connoted between the terms "administration" and "management" as they are used in this chapter. One correspondent points out that the word management came from the Latin *manes ego*, later *manago*, which means to lead by the hand, and that administration came from *administrare*, which means to carry out. Administration thus has a broad meaning, especially in its French usage. It has far more relevance in achieving the purposes of government than in private enterprise. For the purposes of this study the emphasis is on the more action oriented word management or executive management.

Having been tutored by Messrs. Bronlow, Gulick, and Merriam (members of the President's Committee on Administrative Management) and later charged by the director of the budget and President Roosevelt with responsibilities for "administrative management" in the federal government, the author has a bias toward the use of that term. It has elastic connotations, but generally refers to the strategies, processes, and actions that improve administrative capabilities and performance.

Summary

The following findings and proposals are elaborated in later sections of this chapter.

1. Every public executive and manager needs to have an appreciation of, and commitment to, the values and requisites of free and responsible society and to the role of government in serving such needs. The purpose of government was defined by Charles E. Merriam as external security, order, justice, welfare, and freedom. These also re-

quire knowledge of the organs and processes of government, the role of politics and leadership, and the ethics of public responsibility.

2. To discharge executive/managerial responsibilities effectively, three kinds of special knowledge and competence are important in appropriate combinations for different roles.

a. Professional competence in handling the tasks, processes, and relationships inherent in the executive/managerial function, that is, in providing organizational leadership, direction, innovation, productivity, and effectiveness.

b. Intellectual, entrepreneurial, behavioral, interpersonal, and related abilities, traits, motives, maturity, and other characteristics of successful executive managers.

c. Substantive, technological, policy, operational, and contextual knowledge and abilities in the fields or jurisdictions in which the managerial or executive role is carried out.

3. Not many university programs have been designed to develop and strengthen these three categories or clusters of competence in an integrated fashion. However, a few pioneering professional schools of public affairs and administration have been very successful in producing graduates (both preentry and experienced persons) with managerial competence and commitment to public service. Much progress in developing new concepts, reforms, improved methods, and better performance can be attributed to them. These schools are eager to seize on new kinds of managerially focused instructional material to do their job better. Other public affairs/policy schools, and more recently schools of management and schools of business, have a stated or implicit objective of producing graduates for executive/managerial roles in government. Most of these schools lack staff sufficiently interested or experienced in management of government organizations and programs to produce the necessary core and supplemental courses to supply this component.

4. Centers of excellence will not be created unless the school is actually concerned with the administration and operation of federal, state, and local governments and with improving performance in planning and implementing policies and programs. This requires deans, directors, and faculty members who regard these concerns as a primary objective in their own right rather than as an appendage to other work. Unless the school's leadership and instructors are experienced and knowledgeable about government operations and requisites of good management, they will neither have creditability in government circles nor the competence to teach practitioners or prepare others for administrative responsibilities.

5. The U.S. Office of Personnel Management is energetically engaged in strengthening its diversified, government-wide training enterprises. The purpose and content of its executive and management development programs are being attuned to the list of competencies shown in Table 2.1. These are consistent with the three clusters featured in item 2 above. OPM is also setting standards and advising departments and agencies in carrying out their responsibilities for executive and managerial training. Some of these programs are of very high quality. Notable training contributions have also been made by a few state and local governments, professional and public interest groups, nonprofit organizations, and consulting firms.

6. However, a considerable number of officials contacted in this study reported that many training projects to which they have or were requested to assign employees were flimsy. In their opinion these reflect neither good subject matter nor methods. These include both government agency and university programs. Participant enjoyment is not a sufficient basis for evaluation.

7. Academic and short term programs offered by some business schools for public service are well designed and conducted. They appear especially suitable for government employees engaged in public enterprise, or commercial responsibilities, and for those in regulatory agencies, or who otherwise may require knowledge of and contact with the business community.

8. In recognizing the merit of such business type training and that there are some common tasks, processes, and skills, it must also be recognized that public management differs from private business in many fundamental ways. The purposes, political environment, legal constraints, and ambiguities, as well as the values and ethics of public responsibility, are dissimilar. Graham Allison concludes "that public and private management are at least as different as they are similar, and that the differences are more important than the similarities."[2] Clearly, instructional materials used for educating public executives must differ greatly from those applicable to the private sector. Business schools are not appropriate for an appendage of programs designed for the general purpose of preparing public executives and managers.

9. Almost everyone contacted complained about the lack of instructional materials suitable to developing executive and managerial competencies. They pointed out that traditional methods of instruction (lecture, discussion, and reading) are prevalent. Proactive and interactive media designed to maximize mastery of competencies are not well developed or extensively used in many institutions. If better instructional materials and methods become available, it is evident that there would be a splendid market.

Table 2.1 Competencies Deemed Essential for Senior Executives

1. Know agency organization, responsibilities, and role.
2. Know and accept the role of manager.
3. Know and accept the role of the executive.
4. Be able to set objectives and evaluate their accomplishments.
5. Be able to make timely decisions and use appropriate decision-making aids.
6. Be able to establish priorities among alternatives.
7. Be able to develop and implement action plans for the accomplishment of program goals.
8. Be able to develop long-range program plans.
9. Be able to organize resources and structure to accomplish program goals.
10. Be able to effectively delegate.
11. Be able to set individual performance standards and appraise performance.
12. Be able to interact with noncareer managers/executives/staff personnel.
13. Be able to use the basic management support systems in personnel, budget, research and development, EDP/information systems, and procurement.
14. Be able to apply agency personnel policies in key areas such as LMR and EEO.
15. Be able to plan for the adaptation of the organization to a changing environment.
16. Be able to assess own strengths and limitations.
17. Be able to speak clearly and concisely.
18. Be able to write clearly and concisely.
19. Be able to coach and counsel subordinates.
20. Be able to give and receive feedback constructively.
21. Be able to deal with diverse views and ambiguity.
22. Be able to recognize and overcome blocks to communication.
23. Be able to use various leadership styles.
24. Be able to create an organizational climate which results in a motivated workforce.
25. Be able to negotiate on a wide variety of issues.
26. Understand relevant social and political forces.
27. Be familiar with relevant technological developments.
28. Understand general economic conditions and issues.
29. Be able to consider agency policy/programs within the broad context of national priorities.
30. Understand the relationships among and the workings of the Congress, the Office of the President, the executive departments and agencies, and the courts.
31. Understand the relationships between career executives and political executives.
32. Understand the purposes and structure of government as an institution in our democratic society.
33. Recognize the special responsibilities of the public trust.
34. Be familiar with the responsibilities of state and local governments.

Prepared by the U.S. Office of Personnel Management's Task Force on Curriculum Development.

10. Examination of the content and methods of both academic and government programs, as well as experience in designing, teaching, and disseminating management courses, indicates that some very relevant materials and methods are being used. Much of it is designed for

special groups concerned with particular functions and is not developed sufficiently for others to use it in its present form. It is abundantly clear that much more suitable teaching materials and guidance in their use can be prepared and that this would help greatly in improving both degree and nondegree courses.

11. National marketing of instructional packages would encourage governments and their jurisdictional and professional associations to upgrade present officials already in executive/managerial posts or being tagged for such assignments. The users of such materials would be government-wide or agency training centers, universities, and professional or public service institutions. Good materials also have value for individual staff development purposes.

12. A corollary effort should be directed toward preentry professional preparation for talented persons aspiring to undertake a public management career. The impoverished, underdeveloped character of public affairs/administration/management education is not a lack of knowledge but a national failure to support quality institutions and programs. Compared with the national networks of schools of law, agriculture, business, and medicine, public administration/management education has been treated poorly by universities, governments, and foundations.

13. The preparation of several course packages would not produce or constitute a curriculum, either for an academic program or an integrated sequence for nondegree, management development training. They would, however, constitute vital inputs for the management element of a curriculum, perhaps a quarter of a two-year MPA program.

14. Because of the urgent need for such materials, it would be ideal to prepare four or five complementary packages as soon as possible that schools and centers could adapt or cannibalize for specific objectives or clienteles.

15. A competent instructor can readily adapt such materials to focus on administration in particular functions or fields, for example: public health, hospitals, public works, social welfare, energy, environmental protection, community development, school systems, higher education, public enterprise, and urban management. In some cases, such specializations are offered by public affairs/administration schools; in others, by a school of public health, engineering, education, and so forth. Ideally, special packages should be prepared for these purposes.

16. Millions are spent for R&D to develop instructional materials in the various sciences, mathematics, languages, and so forth. Is it not equally or more important to provide those who manage government and its services with basic knowledge and competencies? The compar-

ative contribution or damage that people with each kind of training might make to the future of society warrants thought.

17. If initial possibilities of funding are very limited, preparation of a single course package and guidance for its utilization would demonstrate the value and pave the way for further effort. An initial generic course of high quality could be developed by an experienced person for $30,000 to $40,000. Income from sales should be sufficient to cover cost of printing, marketing, and follow-up.

18. An initial executive management course package should find at least four to five hundred purchasers. If sold for $50 to $75 the income would cover most of the cost of printing and marketing. A somewhat comparable package in the more limited field of intergovernmental policy and program management provides precedent. All 250 copies were sold at $45 by the National Academy of Public Administration.

19. Based on experience with the intergovernmental package (which suffered from inadequate R&D), it would take about six to nine months to prepare a good preliminary edition, and another six months to have a dozen institutions test it, secure feedback, and prepare the copy for the first printed edition.

20. The staggering problems which beset governments at all levels emphasize the need for more capable executives and managers. The crisis in confidence and competence in government is already acute. In comparison, the benefits which would be derived from the kind of instructional materials and methods described in this study would be very substantial. Assignment of funds for this purpose should have much appeal for foundations as well as government support.

INNOVATIVE MANAGEMENT AND ORGANIZATION

Before commenting on the tasks and functions of executives/managers and what they actually do, we should bear in mind the characteristics of the innovation process and what is involved in the creation and management of innovative organizations.

Innovation is the conception, adoption, and implementation of new ideas, methods, or services. Innovative organizations are defined variously as those that "do something they did not know how to do before," "implement new procedures and ideas," "learn to do something new," "make fundamental changes in a significant number of tasks," or are "first or early adopters of ideas."

Innovation results from sustained curiosity: a belief there is always a better way. It requires curiosity, inventiveness, transfer, adaptation, experimentation, negotiation, decision, installation, readjustment, and evaluation. It is risk taking. Before a city, county, state, or national agency can become innovative, it must replace static and slow-moving bureaucracy with dynamic and creative behavior. A signal purpose of executive management education and training is the development of understanding and competence in how to do this. However, fundamental change may be much more difficult to achieve in public organizations than private because it is often contingent upon political support and legislative action.

Characteristics of Innovative Organizations

A resilient and entrepreneurial organization differs significantly from classical, bureaucratic forms. Its structure is more open, flexible, and unstratified. Hierarchy, control, and other monocratic practices are deemphasized. It features consultative and participatory processes. Openness, trust, communication, and cooperation are the mode.

A creative, dynamic organization focuses more on purpose, objectives, and program performance, and less on detailed procedures and job specifications. It fosters esteem versus status striving and changes the reward system from conformity to creativity. It puts a greater premium on professionalism, R&D, and availability of uncommitted money, time, skills, and good will.

Power is widely distributed; responsibilities and inititatives are decentralized. Competition and the casting out of proposals, innovations, and policy issues for wide consideration and resolution are encouraged.

Kinds of Innovation

Becker and Whisler refer to innovation by organizations as a social process involving inputs (predispositions to innovate) and outputs (kinds and values of innovations adopted).[3]

Innovations are of many kinds: objectives, policies, character of product or services, hardware and software technology, procedure and process, structure, human behavior, and relationships. For every public function, activity, profession, specialty, and field of technology application, there are many sources of information on possibilities of innovation. These include organized and self-initiated searches for new concepts, inventions, systems, products, and practices.

All persons in supervisory positions should feel a responsibility for using these sources. This calls for policy mandates, organizational support, acquisition and dissemination procedures, and budget allocations. Development of facilitating individuals and processes is a major task of any executive/manager.

Characteristics of Innovative Managers

In the context of innovation, government executives/managers have been classified in three ways:

custodians of organizations and their maintenance through application of existing levels of knowledge and competence;

improvers of organizational performance, through incremental application of new knowledge and competencies to fields, programs, and operations;

risk taking *innovators* who develop creative organizations characterized by high individual and group generation of innovation, and improved productivity and quality of performance.

Appointment and development of a few innovative executives/managers should strengthen any organization. However, they will be handicapped in changing the character of the organization unless they can enlist converts at lower levels, and surmount external obstacles. Only when they have developed an innovative and participatory work force will there be much organizational innovation with improved performance. This reflects Chester Barnard's mandate of creating a climate in which participants are motivated to meet the system's needs.[4] It is also supported by Rensis Likert's findings that the closer a manager shifts administrative behavior toward a participatory model of management, the more productive the organization becomes and the greater employee satisfaction.[5] This means that public administration/management education and training at all levels should develop a proactive and innovative spirit and competence to spread it.

Systems, styles, and processes of management have great bearing on the innovative behavior of an organization. They largely determine institutional entrepreneurialism and success in idea generation, invention, or transfer; adaptation, adoption, and implementation.

As well as those of a bureaucratic type, there are many other constraints on innovation in government which executives and managers must surmount. These include greater penalties for unsuccessful change, rigid legislative prescriptions, inflexible budgets, difficulty of measuring results (or equivalent of "profit"), and lack of reliable performance evaluation and reward systems. These factors make it more difficult for public administrators to counteract political patronage, favoritism, and interference by legislators and special interest groups.

A Way of Life

Innovation is a form of problem solving with a major additional feature. It requires constant scanning of horizons for better ideas, policies, methods, technologies, behavior, and performance before problems develop.

Inseparable from the demonstration of feasibility is the risk of potential failure and need for commitment of others in the organization as well as of resources. Almost all innovation affects a number of persons, sometimes all, and many existing interdependencies. For this reason, innovation must be made an organizational way of life: an explicit part of every employee's job. Staff units and assistants giving full time to helping line managers engage in innovation assessment, decision, and implementation are a vital auxiliary resource.

Curriculum Implications

Executive/management education and development are obviously concerned to some extent with all these aspects of innovation, especially in ways to achieve creative, responsive organizations. This applies to both academic and nondegree programs.

In the following chapters, Professors Lambright and Doctors suggest what they envision as possible curricula. One or more separate course packages along the lines of their proposals would greatly strengthen any program of executive/management education and development. Some course content proposed by Professor Lambright suggest courses in politics of innovation, economics of innovation, and a course to augment technological literacy.

In a companion chapter, Professor Doctors proposes three core courses for a minor in Public Management of Innovations: (1) Organizational Dynamics, (2) Private Sector Involvement, and (3) Technology Transfer. These courses or minors would be applicable to schools of public affairs and administration, business administration, law, engineering, and in sectoral or functional programs. They should be professional in character, that is, designed to develop operational competencies, not disciplinary in content or method.

If executives/managers are to be buttressed with administrative management assistants and technology advisors to provide staff support in designing, adapting, installing, and operating innovative processes and systems, such persons must be trained for this purpose. A public management innovation curriculum or specialization could help supply and upgrade the requisite personnel. Desirable and important in their own right, such specialties are supplemental to the basic need of developing executives and managers who possess the knowledge, competencies, and personal traits described in the following sections.

THE LEADERSHIP ROLE, FUNCTIONS, AND TASKS OF EXECUTIVES/MANAGERS

Executive and managerial leadership is the single most important factor in creating the administrative capability of a government to perform well. Other necessary elements are: (1) a suitable legal framework, (2) an adequate political mandate, (3) a responsible, well-functioning legislative body, (4) a facilitative organization, (5) effective administrative support services and processes, (6) adequate budgetary resources, (7) high-quality human resources, and (8) competent supervision at all levels.

Resourceful executives/managers can strengthen many of these elements. Others are determined by constitutional, statutory and charter prescriptions, political parties and processes, citizen behavior, and other situational factors.

Sets the Tone

In many ways the leadership abilities and professional competencies of executives/managers set the tone and determine the capability of the organization of subunit for which the executive/manager is responsible. A first-rate person will know how, and be able, to enlist other first rate workers; a second-rate person attracts third-raters; a third-rater convokes fifth-raters.

What is the function of executive leadership and management? What roles, responsibilities, and tasks must be performed? What must an executive/manager know and have competence to do?

A number of studies and much good material is now available for reference by recruiters, curricular developers, and instructors. Since roles and tasks differ considerably for top executives and middle managers, and for different fields and jurisdictions, much interpolation is necessary in examining any explanation or list. Here are a few sketchy hints:

Luther Gulick

The importance of executive management in achieving responsible democratic government was one of the many contributions of Luther

Gulick. Perhaps no other single person has interrelated concept and practice more effectively than he. He elaborated this executive role in the *Papers on the Science of Administration*.[6] One aspect became widely known by the acronym POSDCORB: Planning, Organization, Staffing, Directing, Coordinating, Reporting, and Budgeting.

POSDCORB tasks and processes of administration are by no means obsolete as some behaviorists claim. This view derives from diaries and observations which indicate that executives engage in many fragmented episodes and that they fail to organize their lives around the POSDCORB processes or to be doing things this model reflects.

Gulick's extensive experience as an administrator gave him no illusions in respect to the character of the executive's world. Gulick stressed that (1) these are organizational requisites; (2) the executive is responsible for creating and directing organizations that perform these requisites well; and (3) competent staff as well as line officials are indispensible in this effort.

POSDCORB tasks are only one part of the mosaic of effective and responsible administrative management. They are a vital dimension of management, which will be evidenced by the inadequacies of executives and organizations who overlook them. However, this does not suggest that they comprise more than a fraction of desirable knowledge/competence of good executives. Gulick's view of the executive has always stood in a far broader context.

For example, in his *Administrative Reflections from World War II*,[7] Gulick observed that "we seem to be directing our best young brains into specialized technical and narrow group interests, and leading too few into the integrating techniques and generalized public concerns."

Chester Barnard

Based on his years of executive experience and observation of organizations, Chester Barnard focused more specifically in his writings and speeches in the 1930s on the role of executives. He depicted a leadership role that overarches direction of operations and expertise in special tasks. In the *Functions of the Executive* he emphasized the moral demand upon and accountability of executives for the destiny of their organizations, for communication and seeing that information is shared, for effective relationships, participation, and rewards.[8]

Tasks of Management

A more definitive outline of what government executives/managers are responsible for getting done is reflected in "Tasks of Management," an annotated list developed by the U.S. Bureau of the Budget in consultation with executives ranging from section chiefs to undersecretaries.[9] This author has modified and updated the content over the years in discussions with executives and participants in management development programs. The following are selected capsules:

1. Develop objectives (qualitative and quantitative), priorities, policies, and time and cost parameters.
2. Plan programs to reach objectives, translating each into activities, operations and projects with work plans, schedules, resource needs, and so forth.
3. Plan and build organization structure, including manpower requirements, intraorganizational relationships, and allocated responsibilities.
4. Design and install administrative, operating, and work processes, procedures, and methods.
5. Prepare and translate budget programs into revenue and appropriation requests; allocate funds; and administer finances.
6. Determine staffing priorities and qualifications; recruit and utilize highest skills; train and develop competence; provide good conditions of service; and develop cooperative management-labor relations.
7. Establish management information systems to relate performance and costs to objectives and programs, and to provide a basis for evaluation, control, planning, and policy resolution.
8. Assign responsibilities for analyzing such information to furnish managers, supervisors, and employees with data required for evaluating, adjusting and improving programs, operations, and performance.
9. Motivate the organization through an open participatory management system, two-day communications, fair play and integrity, and concern for employee satisfaction.
10. Maintain effective relationships with employee unions, the legislative body, the media, citizen groups, professional and public interest organizations.

Navy

The Navy Personnel Research and Development Center at San Diego has conducted an informative study of civilian executives.[10] In analyzing how time was spent on fifty work activities, they found that most time was spent on:

1. Providing guidance and direction to subordinates;

2. Taking immediate action in response to crises;
3. Allocating resources (manpower, money, material);
4. Keeping abreast of who is doing what.

NASA

A report by the National Academy of Public Administration for the National Aeronautics and Space Administration on how to develop managers out of scientists and engineers is especially pertinent.[11] The report of the panel, in which I participated, found the most important competencies required by NASA managers to be ability to:

1. Operate within the organization system
2. Operate within the financial system
3. Operate within the personnel system
4. Communicate ideas
5. Coordinate group effort
6. Work with a diversity of people
7. Provide leadership
8. Integrate diverse efforts

Using the report as a guide, NASA created the Management Education Center and developed a superb set of programs for super-grade, presuper-grade, and program/project managers.

Ten Roles

Henry Minzberg in his *Nature of Managerial Work* describes the following ten roles of executives/managers:[12]

Figurehead	Spokesman
Leader	Entrepreneur
Liaison	Disturbance handler
Monitor	Resource allocator
Disseminator	Negotiator

OPM's List

The Office of Personnel Management has prepared a list of thirty-four competencies which it considers essential for senior executives. One aim is to guide curricular development to improve performance by members of the Senior Executive Service and to fulfill grades 14 and 15 management development requirements.

The OPM list, which can be found in Table 2.1, covers general understanding of society and government, managerial knowledge and skills, personal traits, motives, and skills. Many items reinforce and complement the above lists. For example:

Know and accept role of manager

Be able to set objectives and evaluate accomplishments

Be able to use the basic management support systems of personnel, budget, research and development, EDP/information systems, and procurement

Be familiar with the responsibilities of state and local governments

Be able to plan for adaptation of the organization to a changing environment

Understand the relationship among the workings of the Congress, the Office of the President, the executive departments and agencies, and the courts

Understand the purposes and structure of government as an institution in our democratic society

Recognize the special responsibilities of the public interest, and so forth

Canadian attributes

A Canadian government advisory group has made a study of knowledge and skills required of senior managers and executives.[13] The attributes selected are described under the following headings:

1. Expanded Knowledge of the Environment of Executive Performance. This covers governmental, social, cultural, economic, and political.
2. Management and Organization Knowledge. This includes leadership and decision making, financial management, personnel management, program and project management, working relationships, and clientele relationships.
3. Functional Knowledge in one's discipline field and so forth.
4. Personal Capacities and Interpersonal Skills. Examples of this would be coping with stress, time, health, interpersonal relations, team building, group behavior, and leadership.

Recognizing the over-simplification and many exceptions, the advisory group thought in general terms that:

Senior managers tended to look inward, being primarily concerned with departmental affairs.

Senior executives increasingly looked outward, being involved in the relation of their own departmental concerns to those of other departments.

Assistant deputy ministers and deputy ministers (the top career grades) looked upward (as it were) with a concern for their departmental activities in the broad framework of government.

The Public Service Commission is engaged in structuring a continuum of management courses to meet the common core knowledge and skills requirements for the above three classification levels.

AMA's Managerial Focus

The American Management Associations (AMA) offer hundreds of different courses each year to develop professional competencies of private enterprise managers and executives. The keystone is the "Management Course" offered thirty times yearly at varying locations. The competencies stressed are reflected in four weekly units:

Unit I deals with the nature of the managerial job and identifies the fundamental tools managers must acquire before they can carry out any managerial function effectively. They are all relevant to public managers.

Unit II focuses on the major administrative functions of management—setting objectives, formulating policy, organizing, implementing and controlling plans, making financially sound decisions.

Unit III examines in depth what AMA considers the most challenging aspect of management: dealing with people.

Unit IV is concerned with the responsibility of leadership—with how a leader establishes a working environment which encourages voluntary support.

Differentials

The perspectives, functions, and use of time differ considerably among levels of executives, program managers, division chiefs, staff officers, and heads of auxiliary or support services. These differences also apply to professional specialists such as policy analysts, program evaluators, budget reviewers, personnel recruiters, legal counsel, and so forth. Different kinds of organizations, functions, and environments are conditioning factors, albeit there is much common knowledge about administration, organization, policy and program development, and skill in supervising required by all managers in organizations with a hundred or more employees.

Beyond this, several levels of understanding and competencies differentiate the relevant character of education and training for different categories of executives/managers. An illustration of this is shown

Table 2.2. Frank Sherwood's Comparison of the Role of the Manager and the Executive

	Manager	Executive
Orientation	Internally oriented and occupied	Externally oriented; participates in broader system activities as negotiator and representative
General Expectation	To make specific things happen	To create a climate in which things happen
Responsibilities	More homogeneous	More heterogeneous
Resources	Involved in assembling and utilizing resources within a given value context	Involved in allocating resources as a part of setting the value and institutional context
Temporal Perspective	Present—the commitments are relatively short term	Broad perspective to incorporate past and future—the commitments are more apt to be long term
Planning	Programs activity	Serves as conceptualizer and problem solver in a broad range of policy development roles
Directing Activity	Directs operations	Directs through communications and support for key people
Evaluation	Current, in terms of immediate corrections	Post hoc, in terms of learning about future problems and system needs

in the accompanying tabular comparison of the role of managers in the federal government functioning generally at GS-15 and below and that of supergrade executives. It is part of a splendid handout prepared by Frank Sherwood for use in the Executive Roles Workshop of the Federal Executive Institute. The implications on curricula and courses are obvious. (See Table 2.2.)

Plethora of Good Material

Many other studies and commentaries could be cited that provide useful guidance for the curriculum and course developer. For instance, a good description and checklist of management knowledge and competence required of public works executives/managers is found in APWA/NASPAA's *Professional Education in Public Works/Environmental Engineering and Administration*.[14] Other references include Thomas Mahoney's *Building the Executive Team*,[15] the Likerts' *New Ways of Managing Conflict*,[16] Frank Sherwood's FEI handout, "Exploring the Nature of Executive Tasks and Responsibilities in the Federal Government,"[17] and any number of articles.

CHARACTERISTICS OF SUCCESSFUL EXECUTIVES/MANAGERS

The preceding section focused on the functions, tasks, responsibilities, processes, and other work involved in executive and managerial roles. Obviously a person in a sectoral or functional field, such as public works, health, or law enforcement must know or acquire much knowledge about substantive, technological, policy, and programmatic aspects of that field. The farther removed from direct supervision of program and operations, the less important is technical and specialized professional expertise. If lacking in initial appreciation and comprehension, these must be acquired rapidly.

As important as the above kinds of knowledge and competencies may be, the success of an executive or manager ultimately depends on his or her intellectual, behavioral, entrepreneurial, and interpersonal abilities. These involve character traits, motives, self-image, social maturity, and personal skills.

This section is concerned primarily with these latter characteristics and competencies, recognizing that many are interrelated with those stressed in the preceding section. The categorizations are essentially parallel ways of examining managerial behavior. They do have a crucial bearing on the scope and kind of education/training.

Six Sets of Characteristics

For example, in its study of civilian executives, the Navy Personnel Research and Development Center identified the following six sets of characteristics as most important in discharging executive responsibilities:[18]

1. Managerial ability, including the ability to create an effective work environment for subordinates and the ability to plan and direct the work of an organizational unit.
2. Interpersonal skills, involving ability to communicate orally and in writing, listening skills, flexibility, and persuasiveness.
3. Risk-taking ability, including willingness to take risks and to question directives, and having an achievement orientation.

4. Administrative ability, involving the ability to plan, to process paperwork, to act on other organizational demands, and to manage both time and externally imposed crises.
5. Technical skills, including technical ability and keeping up-to-date in one's technical capacity.
6. Awareness of power, entailing survival skills and building a power base.

Stanley's Attributes

David Stanley of the Brookings Institution, in a paper prepared for the National Academy of Public Administration,[19] states that the attributes of top quality managers in order of frequency of emphasis and mention in literature and interviews are: intellectual strength, ability to synthesize, mastery of work content, "political" sensitivity and skill, leadership, development of personnel, and integrity. He says leadership includes unusual energy; is "unflappable" and courteous in crises; listens sympathetically but probingly; has discovered whom to trust; makes this trust evident; uses available incentives with sound judgment based on facts; is contagiously intent upon the organization's goals; and pursues them with enjoyment and tenacity.

HUD's Managerial Competencies

The Department of Housing and Urban Development has isolated several skills or competencies which it considers essential for supervisory and managerial responsibilities. For instance:

1. Coaching and counseling employees
2. Conducting effective meetings
3. Constructive criticism
4. Conflict management
5. Problem solving and action planning
6. Selection interviewing
7. Performance appraisal, interpersonal relations, and system procedures

AMA's Model

The American Management Associations developed a competency model to help in the education and development of successful managers; that is, managers capable of superior performance. Close to 2,000 private and public managers were studied with the help of McBer and Company of Boston over a five-year period. The purpose was to determine competencies that were generic to superior performance. These covered knowledge, motives, traits, self-image, social role, and skills.

The analysis identified eighteen generic competencies grouped into four clusters:

Intellectual Abilities
Logical thought
Conceptualization
Diagnostic use of concepts

Socio-emotional Maturity
Self-control
Spontaneity
Perceptual objectivity
Accurate self-assessment
Stamina and adaptability

Entrepreneurial Abilities
Efficiency orientation
Proactivity

Interpersonal Abilities
Self-presentation
Development of others
Concern with impact
Use of unilateral power
Oral communication skills
Positive regard
Management of groups

This model is focused on middle-level managers. The competencies form a new basis for designing AMA's training programs for middle managers. Management knowledge is not stressed in the model because AMA found that such knowledge is a threshold competency and that most successful managers already grasped it through training and experience. Obviously persons who lack this professional component need to be grounded in it. Training to strengthen the eighteen competencies naturally involves participants in interactive experiences that increases managerial knowledge and skill.

Korn/Ferry—UCLA Study

A different approach to evaluating traits that enhance executive success was used by Korn/Ferry International and a group of UCLA grad-

Table 2.3   Korn/Ferry—UCLA Study Results

Trait	Times Mentioned	Percent
Creativity	763	44.7
Desire for Responsibility	998	57.8
Concern for People	841	49.2
Concern for Results	1259	73.7
Ambition	650	38.1
Integrity	1132	66.3
Loyalty	399	23.4
Aggressiveness	618	36.2
Appearance	252	14.8
Social Adaptability	280	16.4
Exceptional Intelligence	333	19.5
Other Traits	104	6.1

uate students.[20] The study covered 1,708 senior managers in Fortune 500 companies. The respondents were questioned on the traits they thought enhanced their success. (See Table 2.3)

Applicability to the Public Sector

The Korn/Ferry list is confined entirely to private corporations. While oriented primarily to private managers, the AMA model included enough public managers in the sample to show that it has relevance to the public sector. Patently, this would include university administrators, deans, and heads of training units. However, public executives work in more complex environments. They must appreciate the nature of the federal system and be committed to responsible government, rule of law, democratic processes, the public interest, social equity, and the values and ethics of public responsibility.

Public administrators are often confronted with intransigent political, legislative, interest group, and media forces. They are usually accountable for less measurable and controllable programs. They are hemmed in by more prescribed regulations and routines. They are the object of many citizen frustrations for matters for which they have no responsibility or even relationship.

In coping with these contextual constraints and ambiguities, public managers require a wider range of values and competencies. Public management differs from private enterprise in many important ways. A special study by the AMA of public managers and executives in relation to the characteristics and demands of the public sector would be of great value in improving public administration education for public service.

OPM's List

As might be expected, the competencies identified by the U.S. Office of Personnel Management in Table 2.1 reflect these public sector values and environmental characteristics. The OPM list includes a mixture of personal traits and abilities as well as substantive knowledge and professional skills.

OPM's frequent use of the phrase "be able to" reflects a combining of the several kinds of knowledge, abilities, motives, skills, and traits. Persons may "know" but not be able to "do." Some persons are good at "doing" but if they don't know, the results may be disastrous.

One conclusion about education/training to develop these competencies becomes clear. It must be professional and clinical, use resourceful interactive media methods, involve participants emotionally in interpersonal relationships, and deal with what executives and managers need to know and do.

Likert's System 4

An illustration of how good leadership, training, and on-the-job application of these competencies can change behavior and improve performance is shown in applications of Rensis Likert's "participatory management" (system 4) model.[21] Likert and associates have demonstrated that organizations which install and apply the organizational and behavioral requisites or participatory management are both more productive and provide more employee satisfaction than "benevolent authoritarian" (system 2), and especially "punitive authoritarian" (system 1) styles. System 3 is "consultative."

Likert's approach is a feedback data based system of individual and organizational change. The feedback is used continuously to adjust and correct malfunctioning. It provides an operationally effective means of capitalizing on human behavior potential, commonly referred to as "theory Y."

System 4 managers are those who rate high as viewed by their subordinates in the following series of managerial/organization variables or characteristics:

How much confidence and trust is shown in subordinates?
How free do they feel to talk to superiors about their jobs?
How often are subordinates' ideas sought and used constructively?
Is predominant use made of (1) fear, (2) threats, (3) punishment, (4) rewards, and (5) involvement?
Where is the responsibility felt for achieving organization's goals?

How much cooperative teamwork exists?
How much covert resistance to goals is present?
How concentrated are review and control functions?
How well do superiors know problems faced by subordinates?
What is the usual direction of information flow?
How is downward communication accepted?
How accurate is upward communication?
At what level are decisions made?
Are subordinates involved in decisions related to their work?
What does the decision-making process contribute to motivation?
How are organizational goals established?
Is there an informal organization resisting the formal one?
What are cost, productivity, and other central data used for?

An executive who has well-developed traits, motives, and competencies of the kind featured in this section is well equipped to institute system 4 management. Such installations entail training and adjustment of behavior from top executives to first-line supervisors. Some managers are unable to adjust and may need reassignment to nonmanagerial work. With good leadership and a will to succeed, the results are impressive.

Multipurpose

The competency lists or models discussed above and in the preceding section provide criteria for recruitment and promotion as well as education and staff development. Assessment of the extent to which prospects possess predetermined competencies and the potential to acquire them is manifestly a major factor in the selection both for managerial/executive posts and for education/training assignments. However, no amount of managerial education and training will overcome basic inadequacies.

On the other hand, personal competence as well as substantive knowledge can be enhanced by counseling and guided learning experiences. For example, persons with intellectual talent and emotional maturity can greatly increase such AMA featured competencies as perceptual objectivity, entrepreneurial abilities, diagnostic use of concepts, development of others, oral communication skills, and management of groups.

In a broader context, the U.S. Office of Personnel Management has found that senior personnel as well as entrants into the federal service lack understanding of the basic aspects of the U.S. governmental, social, and economic systems. Nor is knowledge of the elements and requisites of administration and management intuitive. The critical tasks confronting federal, state, and local governments in the 1980s surely require a massive strengthening of public service education.

SHORT-TERM, NONDEGREE PROGRAMS

Formal executive/management development courses can contribute significantly to strengthening the managerial competencies and behavior described earlier. Manifestly, no amount of education/training will produce an effective executive out of a depressed introvert or someone incapable of understanding instructions.

Federal Specifications

The U.S. Office of Personnel Management describes the following components in its specifications for agency executive development systems:

Determine type and competencies of executive posts
Recruit widely and select on merit basis
Assess individual competencies and prepare individual development plans
Provide continuing development opportunities in accordance with individual plans

Development opportunities include policy updating seminars; OPM sponsored executive training; agency training and university programs; on the job work; special assignments; task force opportunities; periodic inhouse short-term sessions; scheduled coaching; performance appraisal; temporary, mobility, and rotation assignments; and central reporting, appraisal, and oversight.

Overcoming Resistance

During recent years some first-rate executive/management training centers and courses have been created. Federal departments and OPM are now engaged in developing and strengthening both executive/management systems and formal training programs. These provide valuable resources for the design of instructional materials as well as a ready-made market for utilization of newly packaged materials and guidance in instructional methods.

While there is greater commitment to executive/managerial training and development than ever before, several obstacles must be overcome. An assistant secretary for administration commenting on this project says:

Many educational and training courses are of low quality. Busy people do not like to waste time.

Organizational pressures and incentives to take training are lacking.

Political executives who supervise career executives and managers are not themselves managers except by title and hence neither appreciate nor encourage organizational or individual efforts toward executive development.

He also comments that in a time of budget retrenchment, training is one of the easiest items to delete. It has no special interest lobbies.

The following are illustrative of nondegree, executive/management development programs that can be involved in producing and using packaged materials.

The Federal Executive Institute. Established in 1968 by the U.S. Civil Service Commission, the Federal Executive Institute (FEI) has become the government's principal center for training of supergrade (Senior Executive Service [SES]) personnel and GS-15s in a pre-SES status. It features a seven-week Senior Executive Education Program. Some state and local executives are also enrolled.

FEI's three-week Executive Leadership and Management Program now enrolls GS-15s in approved agency executive development programs and other persons holding significant managerial positions. SES attendance is limited to 25 percent. FEI courses focus on many of the competencies described in the previous sections.

OPM Executive Seminar Centers. First initiated in 1962, three regional centers provide new managers as well as old hands in GS-13 through 15 with supervisory and managerial competencies needed at this level of leadership responsibility. Their courses deal with more specialized fields of management than FEI's. OPM also operates a couple of institutes in Washington which provide management programs of a week or less for GS-13 to 15, with some SES participants.

OPM's Office of Training. Five training centers sponsored by this office offer many diverse courses to state and local as well as federal officials. It also develops and supplies instructional materials for departments and agencies. The centers are engaged in many innovative undertakings.

NASA Management Education Center. This residential center is an excellent example of agency effort. Three programs were designed to implement NAPA's recommendations referred to in the preceding section: (1) a middle management education program for GS-14s and 15s, (2) a senior program for super-grades, and (3) a special program for project managers. The substance is excellent.

The 1980 announcement of NASA's thirteenth offering of its three-week program for midlevel managers stresses opportunities for participants to:[22]

Examine their style and methods of managing
Improve their managerial knowledge and skill
Examine their role in a changing NASA environment
Broaden their understanding of NASA as a system of interdependent programs, offices and centers

HUD's approach. The Department of Housing and Urban Development has initiated two major efforts to improve capacity to meet organizational goals. One is the Leadership Training and Development System (LTD) for supervisors and managers. The other is the Executive Development Program. LTD is competency based and skill oriented with testing to measure results. The skills and competencies currently featured are listed on page 31. These skills are designed to aid in the development of human resources for quality and quantity production in meeting HUD's program objectives.

At the executive level, HUD uses the assessment center method to select high potential individuals. After final selection the individual is given several rotation assignments notably in field offices. Supplementary executive development opportunities then become available.

The Defense Management Education and Training Catalogue.[23] This 289 page document provides guidance for officers and civilian officials who select individuals from the Department of Defense and the armed services for training. The variety and level of management focused courses is extraordinary, dwarfing in relative terms the efforts of any civilian department.

Defense Systems Management College. This college (located at Fort Belvoir) is a splendid illustration of creative efforts of the Department of Defense to increase managerial capabilities. The purpose of the college is to develop officers and civilians capable of planning, producing, and managing complex weapons systems. It demonstrates the value of buttressing innovative training programs with research and publications. The latter provide follow-on activity and contribute to operational guidance as well as to continuous improvement of instruction. The college provides a model worthy of emulation by other government training centers.

FBI Academy. The FBI Academy is especially notable for its exceptional funding and physical quarters. Executive/management development and education support by presidents (OMB) and the Congress for civil servants is dismal compared with military and paramilitary services. Defense of the country and its people appears important but not the quality of their survival.

Other federal training. Training work which should also be examined in any effort to develop packages of instructional material includes the Internal Revenue Service, Veterans Administration, General Accounting Office, Federal Acquisitions Institute, and several departments notably State, Health and Human Services, and Housing and Urban Development.

Professional and public interest groups. Some of the best management training courses for public officials are provided by the National Institute of Public Affairs (an organ of the National Academy of Public Administration), the International City Management Association, National League of Cities, United States Conference of Mayors, American Public Works Association, and similar organizations. In many cases either the programs or individuals are assisted by federal funding.

The International City Management Association has the longest and most resourceful record of management education. It began its "green book" extension courses in the early 1930s. It produces instructional packages, conducts courses, and maintains linkages with universities. Its national and state conferences are substantial management development experiences.

IPA funded programs. A substantial increase in state and local government management training has been generated by Intergovernmental Personnel Act funds administered by the U.S. Office of Personnel Management.

An example is Georgia's Certified Public Manager Programs. This is a cooperative enterprise of the Training and Development Division of the State Merit System of Personnel Administration and the University of Georgia's Institute of Government. The curriculum consists of six levels of defined objectives and subjects covering many of the traits, motives, competencies, skills, and knowledge covered in earlier sections. Examinations leading to certificates are featured at four stages. Successful completion of the four results in the participant being designated a "certified public manager."

The Georgia program has been so well conceived that it is serving as a model for other states. The National Training and Development Service (sponsored by the seven major public interest groups) now has an IPA grant to assist applications in five states.

In this context, the dean of a school enrolling several hundred mid-career officials wrote "The feds have their several major training places. State and local governments do not. What I would like to see before too long is a state taking the initiative to develop a staff college for state and local government. Then the packages would have the most utility."

AMA's Professional Institute. This special branch of the American Management Associations provides specially staffed and designed programs to increase managerial effectiveness in the public and non-profit sectors. It features courses and seminars for (1) federal, state, and local executives; (2) managers in selected functional fields such as health, education, and criminal justice; and (3) staff of religious, charitable, and other nongovernmental organizations.

Courses reported to be most valuable are "Essentials of Management," "Improving your Managerial Effectiveness," "Strategic Planning Processes," "Time and Productivity Management," "Finance for Non-financial Executives," "Top Management Briefings," and "Management by Objectives." Some courses designed for a specific organization also concentrate on special subjects such as "Standards of Performance," "Project Management," "Information Management," and "Zero-Based Budgeting."

Center for Creative Leadership. This nonprofit foundation supported institution located in Greensboro, North Carolina, is devoted to improving the practice of management. Through research on what managers do and what competencies they require, the center develops training programs to provide people at critical levels of organizational responsibility with better ways to recognize leadership potential, and to develop and fully utilize human resources.

Currently, the center's work is focused on five areas: creative leadership, personal effectiveness, managerial effectiveness, organizational effectiveness, and research and training methodologies.

The center studies how a creative leader may differ from an effective leader and whether the qualities are trainable. One aim is to discover how managers can achieve organizationally relevant goals with a minimum of unwanted psychological disruption within work groups. A related question being researched and reflected in training is the capacity of managers and organizations to recognize and adapt constructively to environmental changes and to meet organizational goals. This is viewed as the central issue or organizational effectiveness.

The principal offerings of the center are five- and seven-day leadership development programs. The brochure states that these begin with personal assessment as the foundation of a process of self-development. The focus of the training is on creative leadership, decision making, leadership styles, utilizing group resources, creative problem solving, and the art of feedback and counseling. This self-development process continues with the setting of individual goals and aspirations. The center appears to be an ideal resource for assistance in preparation of packages.

University nondegree programs. A considerable number of schools of public affairs/administration offer short-term, intensive or intermittent programs for public officials.

For example, Harvard's Kennedy School of Government has launched nondegree programs emphasizing the management component of public policy. These are designed for such groups as senior managers in government, national and international security managers, state and local executives, and environmental and health policy managers. A new venture slated for this fall is a thirteen-week Senior Executive Fellows program aimed at top candidates for entry into the U.S. Senior Executive Service.

Not many schools appear to feature a broad cross section of managerial competencies depicted in preceding sections. They tend to concentrate on special processes, analyses, and interpersonal skills: for example, human relations, communications, policy analysis, program evaluation, decision making, management information systems, organizational development, labor-management relations, coping with executive stress, budgeting and finance, personnel administration, the computer and quantitative methods, or some combination. Others are designed for public health, law enforcement, community development, human resource, and other specialized personnel.

Interestingly, some of these nondegree courses are far better structured to develop previously described competencies than the school's master's programs. They use practitioner-oriented instructors, whereas master's courses are largely taught by theorists, analysts, and persons primarily interested in disciplinary research.

Some business schools also enroll government officials in courses designed for business executives. Many have good managerial content but are not usually related to public functions and conditions. At least three business schools have designed attractive programs specifically for public executives.

Continuing education programs offered by extension divisions or comparable units generally cover a potpourri of anything describable. They often include courses on public administration and management. Many are organized without much R&D and are taught in a classical lecture and discussion format. Often the main purpose is to produce income for the organization offering the course.

Market for new material. A sufficient check has been made to determine that high quality instructional materials designed for these short term nondegree programs would have a good market. Several heads of centers said the most critical need is for proactive/interactive problem-solving projects, real or simulated, that equate the realities of operating situations.

Often those institutions which appear to have first-rate programs expressed the greatest interest in having access to new materials. If instructors charged with teaching these auxiliary courses for mid-career personnel learned that they could secure such materials organized for selective use in immediately usable form, there would be much interest. Ability to save time in the development and refinement of their courses with tested materials would be the most persuasive inducement.

UNIVERSITY DEGREE PROGRAMS

Many of the 200 member institutions of the National Association of Schools of Public Affairs and Administration are good prospects for use of better instructional materials. These institutions vary greatly in objectives, scope, clientele, curriculum, and sophistication. About thirty or forty are comprehensive schools, that is, genuinely multidisciplinary and professional with status in university structure comparable to schools of business and law.

Some of the 200 institutions comprise departments in social science or liberal arts colleges. Others are units or specializations in schools of business or management, or departments in combined schools of business and public administration. In the 1970s a number of public policy schools came into being which stress the acquisition and application of analytical methods. Many programs confined within the single discipline of a political science department currently utilize little, if any, management course work of the kind proposed here.

Examination of catalogues of these institutions reveals relatively little instruction designed to provide the knowledge and competencies outlined earlier. The principal courses of many institutions, particularly the political science based programs, tend to be descriptive, theoretical, research oriented, or cover two or three special aspects of administration such as personnel, finance, policy analysis, and research methods.

Predominant Subjects

This is vividly borne out in a study by the Virginia Commonwealth University of subjects taught and text books used by fifty-five universities with MPA programs.[24] The following are the principal courses (often core requirements) in common use:

Introduction to Public Administration
Statistics and Research Methods
Evaluation and Policy Analysis
Organization Theory
Management Theory
Personnel Administration
Administrative Law
Public Sector Economics
Public Financial Management

Some NASPAA member institutions offer programs that have even fewer public administration courses. The comprehensive schools have far more coverage and generally provide a number of specializations. Very few institutions offer clinically intensive management courses or use proactive instructional methods in courses like those listed above. Upon receipt of syllabi and illustrations of instructional materials and projects I have used, the Virginia Commonwealth project director telephoned to report that it was the first submittal out of thirty-eight up to that time which dealt with management from a professional or practitioner's standpoint.

Causes and Consequences

MPA graduates appear to be equipped to converse about administration and to analyze problems, but not to do much operationally. This is similar to a medical school producing surgeons by having them read

books on the history of surgery, anatomy, and physiology, or by learning the names and purposes of surgical facilities and equipment.

Schools of business, which increasingly publicize administra-
tion/management options, put more stress on management, but most
of it is taught in a business context. Some combined schools, or schools
of management, provide bridges—some pretty shaky—between the
public and private sectors.

Schools of public policy tend to assume that good policies or analytically determined program options are self-implementing. Mastery of
analytical methodologies, particularly quantitative skills, has been
viewed as prime qualification for executive/managerial roles.

At the start of a school or program plan, the new head and associates usually have considerable flexibility to design a curriculum with
some relationship to the market and, in turn, to produce an end product with operationally applicable competencies. Once professors are in
place with predominantly single disciplinary and methodological interests, the curriculum becomes a collection of negotiated concur-
rences for teaching individual interests. Many a dean has despaired
after securing commitment for a practitioner-oriented course to find
that the instructor paid little attention to that stated purpose, but
rather lectured on his/her specialized interest.

One lesson is that the head and dominant faculty of a professional
school of public affairs/administration/policy must be multidisciplinary and practitioner oriented. Unless such persons also have a major
interest in the administration of government and management policies, functions and institutions, the school will not produce preservice
or inservice graduates with executive/managerial competencies.

In making this review of present practices, it should not be assumed
that graduate education in public affairs, administration, or management is a prerequisite for executive/management posts. Governments
find talent in many places with many backgrounds. Many persons acquire the knowledge and competencies described in previous sections
on the job, and in ways other than formal training. Most managers
move into administrative responsibilities after a period of specialized
professional or technical work. However, all should obviously benefit
by midcareer management training opportunities. If university programs were more relevant, their resources would be far more extensively utilized.

Forces for Change

Several developments suggest that the time is ripe for substantial readjustment in university curricula. Increased publicity is being given

to the need for relating those university programs that aspire to prepare their graduates for executive and management responsibilities to the kinds of knowledge and competencies outlined in previous sections.

Government executives and managers and their personnel systems are increasingly in search of persons who possess the kinds of knowledge and competencies described. They will naturally be on the lookout for capable persons who have been engaged in public management education, preferably as a capstone or supplement to other relevant professional education and experience. James Sundquist's article in the January 1979 issue of *Public Administration Review* appraising Jimmy Carter as an administrator and citing the consequence of poor management shows the importance of this.[25]

Establishment of the Senior Executive Service and the mandate for OPM and departments to establish executive/management development opportunities is forcing more attention to the competencies featured herein in appointments, promotion, and performance evaluation throughout the entire federal government. Not only will the government give greater priority in the future to professionally educated management talent, but agencies are already developing linkages with some universities responsive to change.

This national thrust is contagious. State and local governments are stepping up their efforts to recruit, develop and reward executive management talent. If ways are found to move incompetent and mediocre incumbents out of executive/managerial posts, the number of better trained persons that can be utilized is astronomical.

An increasing proportion of the students enrolled in schools of public affairs/administration are officials working for master's degrees and doctorates in part-time study. Some of the large schools with a management component, such as New York University, American, University of Southern California, Kennedy, Golden Gate, and the University of Pittsburgh have a dominant midcareer component. These and many other institutions are actively searching for instructional material.

Many heads of university programs are aware of a managerial deficiency in their curriculum, but they do not know what to do about it. Once guidance and instructional material is publicized, they will be fortified. If a practitioner-oriented instructor competent to teach a new course is not already on the faculty, an experienced practitioner with appropriate academic qualifications can be appointed as an adjunct professor. Every faculty needs several such persons.

This has been the experience with the Curriculum Package on Intergovernmental Management. As soon as deans, professors, and directors of government-training programs received the prospectus, they saw the merit of its coverage and clinical projects. They also had the reassurance of its previous testing by a dozen reputable schools. Soon the word spread that it saved enormous time and effort in organizing a new course and in adapting existing courses to more practical use. It became a sell-out.

The standards for master's programs issued by the National Association of Schools of Public Affairs and Administration stress public administration knowledge, skills, and values. With the emerging interest of governments in executive, managerial, and implementation competencies, these standards will inevitably give more attention to their acquisition.

Obstacles to Change

Two roadblocks to changing curricula are prevalent. The first is frequent subordination of what should be multidisciplinary based professional programs in single disciplinary departments of political science or in schools of business.

The second problem is the manner in which curricula and courses are determined, even in independent schools of public affairs and administration. Most instructors have their Ph.D.'s in a discipline. They are largely interested in the substance and analytical methods of their disciplines. Many lack a professional/practitioner focus and thus have little knowledge or interest in management, even though it is the central ingredient of public administration and of public policy development and implementation. They give little if any thought to the competencies outlined in the previous sections.

This generalization appears increasingly relevant to graduate schools of business. Their faculties, too, are becoming saturated with model builders and analytical methodologists. A reflection of this is the highly publicized and vacuous rating of top business schools. Since most professors have more interest in methodology and special subjects than in management, it is not surprising that higher ratings tend to be given to schools which are analytically focused rather than to those which are managerially oriented.

The real question is whether students are exposed to the practical side of public management as well as the theoretical. Analysis is a technique. Management is a subject or field of practice. Since skilled analysts are much needed, some institutions should make a much needed contribution by producing superior analysts highly versed in the development and use of various methodologies. The aim, however, of any professional school should be to produce graduates who will work in the real world and to equip them with the most applicable competencies. If the purpose is to produce public executives and managers, that is a different matter. Technical skill in using advanced analytical techniques becomes secondary. Obviously, they need to know about the potential uses of analytical processes and the computer and interpretation of results.

The demise of the Fels Institute of State and Local Government at the University of Pennsylvania supplies a worthy lesson. For years this dynamic institution with a primary focus on management channeled far more graduates into city manager and other urban and state administration posts than any other university. Their successful careers gave Fels a legendary reputation. Then the University decided to follow the fad. It replaced the curriculum with an advanced set of courses in economic and other analytical methods. The loss to the country is considerable.

The Kennedy Example

Recent developments in the John F. Kennedy School of Government illustrate how one of the oldest schools is reversing this trend. It is particularly significant since the original curriculum of the Littauer School of Public Administration contained almost no administration and management subject matter. Later the analytically focused public policy program became a lead product.

The school has now restructured its curriculum to inject into its public policy program a substantial political/managerial component. Moreover, public policy, as well as midcareer, students may major in public management. Table 2.4 shows the new format.

In both academic and varied special programs for public officials, the Kennedy School stresses development of political, policy, implementation, ethical, interpersonal, and other managerial competencies. This has involved additions to its faculty of public administration and public management generalists and practitioners, with redesignations of old titles to reflect managerial thrust. Any institution desiring to improve its public affairs/administration/policy curriculum and faculty will be well advised to examine the Kennedy catalogue.

AMA Master's Proposal

A second illustration is the decision of the American Management Association to seek approval of the New York Board of Regents to offer a master's degree in management. The initial program will enroll tal-

Table 2.4.   Courses Offered by the Kennedy School of Government

Kennedy School courses begin on September 17 in the Fall, and on January 28 in the Spring.

The following course numbers and special symbols apply to the Kennedy School's courses:

P: Public Policy Core Curriculum

P-100-199 Open only to first-year candidates for the Master's Degree in Public Policy.

P-200-299 Open only to second-year candidates for the Master's Degree in Public Policy.

The following courses are open to all KSG students, unless limited by size of enrollment or by prerequisites:

M: Methods and Principles

M-100-399 Analytics
M-400-499 Political Analysis
M-600-799 Public Management
M-800-899 Ethics
M-900-999 Practice in Public Policy Analysis and Design

S: Substantive Areas

S-100-149 Energy and Environmental Policy
S-150-174 Human Resources
S-175-199 Health Policy
S-200-249 International Affairs and Security
S-250-269 Transportation
S-270-349 Government and Business
S-350-399 Criminal Justice
S-400-499 Science and Public Policy
S-500-574 International Development
* * * *   State and Local Policy and Management

Students interested in taking courses on state and local policy and management should refer to the course cluster foldout (yellow pages).

R: Reading and Research

R-100-499 Reading and Research
R-500-999 Direction of Doctoral Dissertation

Special Note. KSG courses have been given new identification numbers for 1979-80. For those who remember courses by their earlier designation, a conversion table appears on page 148, at the end of the course listings.
Credit. Half course, full course and modular course.
A normal course load is eight half courses per year (four per semester). Two half courses equal one full course, and two modules equal one half course.

Modular Courses. Modular courses meet during four "periods" of the year. The four periods are:

Period I: September 17-November 9
Period II: November 12-January 11
Period III: January 28-March 21
Period IV: March 31-May 16

Symbols. Following is an explanation of course-related symbols:

m   A modular course is identified by a lower-case "m" following the course number.
hf   A half course meeting throughout the year (usually every other week) is designated by an "hf" following the course number.
a, b Half courses which form a logical sequence use the same number but add lower case "a" and "b" to distinguish them from one another and to indicate the order involved. Students wishing to enroll in a "b" course without having taken the corresponding "a" course must have the permission of the instructor.
[ ]   A course number and title enclosed in brackets indicates that the course is not being offered during the current year.
( )   A day enclosed in parentheses indicates that the course meets on that day only at the pleasure of the instructor.
TBA   Information to be announced. See the bulletin board outside the Registrar's office for further notice, or inquire of the Registrar.
_____   A blank line where the instructor's name should appear signifies an instructor yet to be announced.

Source: Taken from the course catalogue of the Kennedy School of Government.

48

ented middle managers in a curriculum designed to strengthen the eighteen competencies in AMA's model described in an earlier section.

AMA's prospectus states:[26]

> MBA programs (applies equally to MPA) are input oriented, that is, they assemble Ph.D. faculties, high test scoring students, large libraries, etc. The assumption is that with high quality inputs, there will be high quality output. Research has shown this is not the case. AMA has an output orientation, that is . . . we are much concerned with helping students acquire the knowledge and some intellectual skills. AMA program relies on proactive teaching media and also teaches knowledge, but the emphasis is on teaching 18 skills, including the intellectual skills.

In another section the prospectus comments:

> Because skills are best "learned by doing," delivery of the Master of Management program will incorporate many new proactive educational techniques such as games, simulations, leaderless groups, computers, role plays, etc.

Conclusions

The favorable forces for accelerating an executive management component by schools interested in this objective are considerable and enduring. Universities will respond if federal, state, and local governments directly, or through public interest and professional associations, will make increasingly clear what is wanted and give more financial inducements to secure a better product. The preparation of packaged instructional material and guidance will enable them to move rapidly and effectively.

The guidance component should show the mutually supportive and contributory benefits derived from interrelating action-oriented research, advisory assistance, and nondegree programs with a graduate curriculum. It should also be made clear that to attain both excellence and acceptance by government employers, a school desiring to prepare preservice and inservice persons for managerial responsibilities must possess a practitioner-oriented faculty. There must be a dominant concern with the real world of government. A person without commitment to and experience in governmental management would hardly make a successful or acceptable instructor regardless of the utility of a course package.

These conclusions lead to the recommendation that the federal government foundations, or any person concerned with improving public management underwrite a program to give guidance in curricular and course development with a variety of clinically based instructional packages to meet discrete needs. The OPM is a suitable organ but it lacks funds. If the National Science Foundation can demonstrate the feasibility and value by commissioning prototype projects and thus lay the basis for an expanded and continuous effort, it will help fulfill its mandated objectives in serving an acute and important national need. In view of what the Advisory Commission on Intergovernmental Relations refers to as a "crisis of confidence and competence," such a program should appeal to foundations or to any organization or person concerned with the ability of the federal system to cope with present and emerging problems.

ACIR in a monumental study of how the federal system is working finds that it is doing badly.[27] It points to (1) administrative failures, red tape, and tensions between levels of government; (2) poor performance and inadequate results; (3) excessive costs and waste; and (4) lack of adequate control and responsiveness through political process.

Clearly government at all levels requires a capacity for administrative leadership, policy development, and program management far superior than what now exists. Development and widespread use of the kind of curricula and courses proposed here is indispensable in any effort to improve performance.

PREPARATION OF COURSE PACKAGES

The findings reported in previous sections reveal a critical need for preparation of instructional materials which focus on executive/managerial functions, competencies, and behavior. Seldom has such unanimity of views been found among public officials, professional and public interest associations, and academics on the feasibility of an important innovation. Since the market for such materials is related to costs of production, these twin questions are covered in the following section.

Complementary Packages

Clearly of most value would be optional or complementary course packages containing modules, scenarios, background analyses and textual resources, clinical projects (proactive media exercises), and guidance in their use. They should be flexible and as adaptable as possible to different jurisdictions, fields/functions, markets, and kinds of participants.

The reason several packages are proposed is that the subject matter, fields/functions of application, jurisdictional situations, and competencies to be developed are so varied. Diversity is also necessary to support a curriculum in public administration/management as well as to supply government training centers and university nondegree programs with a sufficient choice of directly relevant material.

One requisite stands out above all others. The scenarios and content should rely on proactive and interactive media involving simulations and other problem-solving situations. That should be the main character of the learning experience, and should force participants to draw on and apply the kinds of knowledge and behavior described in previous sections. Emotional involvement is essential to change attitudes and behavior. Lecturing and use of traditional textbooks are not a suitable means to achieve this result.

Feasibility of a Generic Package

To get started, it is feasible to develop a single demonstration package which focuses on basic and generic knowledge and competencies. If designed in a manner to facilitate flexible use, an experienced and resourceful instructor can adapt the material and projects to fit different clientele and situations.

Materials suitable for an academic course can be cannibalized for midcareer, short-term training. Naturally, packages would be much more useful if designed specifically for the participants—senior executives and managers as well as the mixed composition that characterizes most master's courses.

The title suggested for an initial package is "Executive Leadership and the Function of Management." Preparation of a single package is only a stop gap—a means of demonstrating. Additional packages should interrelate knowledge and competencies discussed earlier in a manner to serve an ascertained diversity of market needs. For example, some subject areas proposed below for the initial package warrant expansion in some combination into additional packages. A package somewhat comparable in scope to an initial generic package should focus on "Urban Executive Management."

Specially designed materials are much needed for sectors or functions such as public health, hospitals, public works (or subfields such as transportation, water resources, energy, environmental protection), education, law enforcement, and so on. Public enterprise and university administration are combinations of the two types.

Such courses may be offered in MPA concentrations or in specialized professional schools such as engineering, public health, and social work/services.

In jurisdictional and sectoral focused packages, the content and guidance material can be far more specifically related to the substance, technology, policies, administrative characteristics, culture, and environment of the field.

Package Content

Course packages should contain several elements.

1. An explanation of purpose and organization of materials; adaptation to a curriculum core or advanced academic offering; ways of cannibalizing for short-term courses; application to functional fields; method of updating materials; inductive teaching and other requisites for effective learning experience designed to change behavior; basis for grading or evaluation of performance; physical setting; selection of students/participants; situational adjustments; feed back evaluation and revision, and so forth.
2. Outline of modules/packets, including applicable clinical projects.
3. Modular packets for each topic containing:
   Explanation of objectives
   Scenario, background comment, discussion issues and other information to be provided students/participants, together with project assignments, and handout textual items.
   Instructor's guide which suggests classroom scenarios, method of conducting workshop sessions, handling of projects to secure effective interaction, points to be stressed, lessons to be learned, use of subgroups, project reports, and ways to provide an effective learning experience.
   Project critiques suggesting conclusions and generalizations to be drawn inductively, how the project could have been performed better, and how to respond to something comparable on the job situations.
4. Concluding wrap-up session, course evaluation, recognition of effort, presentation of certificates, and so forth.
5. Follow-on application of what has been learned.

Initial Package

The initial generic package would be most adaptable if designed as a one semester core course for use in any kind of master's or doctoral curriculum in public affairs, administration, management, or policy studies. The proposed method of organizing the package will facilitate selection of useful parts for government training and short-term programs or workshops of a few hours or weeks. It could be drawn upon in the same way to shore up existing academic courses.

Attached to this section is a very preliminary outline of topics or modules for a course package of this character, tentatively titled "Executive Leadership and the Function of Management." The suggested title is similar to a course incorporated in the core course program serving several fields or concentrations at the Graduate School of Public and International Affairs, University of Pittsburgh. The last time it was taught at Pitt, the course was labeled "Executive Management in Achieving Policy and Program Objectives." Alternate titles might be "Executive Leadership and Management," or "Executive Management of Innovative Organizations."

Adaptability

To serve the needs of both experienced and inexperienced students, the materials should be designed primarily for persons with considerable background and up to middle-level management responsibility. This will in fact improve their value for students with little practical experience, although such students should be of high quality and preferably at an advanced graduate level. This kind of learning experience is precisely what they need. The rigor of the materials can easily be modified. However, its professional and clinical character should be fully maintained. Too many courses offered in MPA programs are essentially disciplinary and subprofessional in character. A good way for professional students to learn about the relevance of disciplines is to assign them problems which require use of disciplinary knowledge and methods.

The inclusion of persons with different levels of experience in an academic course does not create as much of a problem as many assume. The main requirement is that the course content be suitable for the more experienced. The less experienced will learn from them. Any class of recent graduates benefits greatly by enrolling two or three experienced older persons. The instructor's skill naturally makes a big difference.

This flexible use is enhanced by incorporating optional material in the package. The proactive media problem-solving exercises or projects offer a good opportunity to do this. Some can be equally appropriate for preentry graduate students as for public officials. In many cases dealing with the same subject or problem, optional projects are needed. In some instances the project assignments may need to differ as to subject and problem.

Application to Fields of Interest

A resourceful instructor can also give this flexible kind of course package special relevance to participants concerned with different fields. One way is to have each student select a field of specialization. By focusing their readings, projects, and field work (including internship) on their primary field of interest, students can develop considerable knowledge and marketable competencies. This principle is applicable to many courses in any public affairs/administration/policy curriculum.

A second way is for the instructor to use cases and examples inductively and to draw parallels and contrasts in applications among different fields. Administration is not conducted in a vacuum, and should always be related in course work to jurisdiction, function, and other contextual aspects.

The Real World

Implicit in the above is the utilization of both background material and projects to immerse participants in the realities of the administrative and political world. The common indictment made by officials and persons who have earned master's degrees is the lack of practitioner orientation and the use of models and cases which has little practical use.

A former official now conducting university short-term training writes: "One of the weaknesses that I noted as MPAs joined HEW was their lack of understanding of bureaucratic roles and activities. It took most of them six months to a year to become functional."

The value of the proposed packages in overcoming this handicap is attested by another respondent: "You vividly map the chasm between the typical academic program in public affairs/administration and the real world curriculum you propose. . . . Traditional programs are not seen by managers as relevant . . . these programs really generate specialists in policy analysis, for instance, rather than leaders and managers."

Limited Coverage

The proposed course covers a considerable range of executive management responsibilities. Any student exposed to this kind of workshop should have a potent learning experience. Based on evaluations by students of such subject matter and projects, the course would be rated as one of the best. However, it must be recognized that what can be covered in one course is a small part of an adequate managerial component. The subjects and exercises tentatively suggested are a fraction of those desirable in both university and government training programs. Some of the projects would require more than a week. That is why several complementary courses are needed.

The course outline assumes one three-hour or two one-and-one-half-hour sessions on the average for each topic combined with classroom work on projects. Fourteen or fifteen three-hour or thirty one-and-one-half-hour sessions are the usual maximum in a semester. Seventeen modules are suggested to give an instructor choice, and to recognize that some subjects may be covered in other courses. The time available for topics, project work, and critiques will always be limited. An enterprising instructor could convert the course into a two-semester sequence, or divide and combine with other subjects into two distinct courses.

Projects

The projects listed in the following syllabus are only illustrative. Considerable sleuthing and invention will be needed to develop a good collection. For most purposes the use of group interaction in dealing with simulated situations and empirical investigation provide better experience-based learning than lengthy cases, especially when there is much to cover. To be of much value, cases must be handled by a clever instructor to secure intensive interaction among participants in dealing with realistic and managerial focused situations.

The package should also provide for the use of videotapes and films with suggestions for their use in a manner which enables reaction and application. As in the use of cases, participant interaction in functioning in a managerial role is the name of the game. Projects and videos can make good use of experienced practitioners and experts. For example, the legislative roles in a hearing can be dramatized by inviting outsiders.

Training of Instructors

If proactive materials are to be used and related to the practitioner's world, considerable retooling of instructors is essential. This underlines the value of recruiting instructors who have been educated in or have applied their interests to public management.

The package should contain considerable guidance on how to use the material, conduct the projects, and in the use of inductive methods to maximize benefits. Instructors who used the intergovernmental management package reported that it was a splendid learning experience for them and for developing their teaching competency.

ESTIMATED TIME, COSTS, AND MARKET

The cost of preparing instructional packages will vary depending on the character of the audience and field, the level of sophistication, and the availability of relevant materials. The biggest variable is the discovery of competent persons or organizations experienced in this kind of effort. Some have been identified in the course of this study.

Range of Costs

For example, a package for super-grade level management development containing optional materials for fifteen to twenty full days of residential use should warrant an investment of $100,000. This would provide complementary materials in a form for instructional use to those now used by the Federal Executive Institute, mainly for departmental, state-wide, and university use, and for courses offered by professional and public interest organizations.

Another example is a two-semester sequence in public works management for core instruction short-term and graduate programs to implement the joint recommendations of the American Public Works Association and the National Association of Schools of Public Affairs and Administration. The two packages might be prepared for $70,000 to $90,000 provided materials in the initial generic package could be adapted and used as a model.[28]

A package designed for preentry students in a master's program could be produced at much less cost than the super-grade version, or one which recognizes that experienced persons comprise all or some portion of the enrollment. The former would require less creation of new and optional material.

Cost of Initial Package

A highly innovative, generic demonstration package with considerable adaptability as previously outlined would warrant R&D of $50,000 to $60,000, or more. A good package with fewer project op-

Table 2.5   Illustrative Modules for a Course Package in Executive Leadership and the Function of Management

1. The changing characteristics of U.S. intergovernmental, international, political, and environmental complexities with which the executive/manager must contend.

    Project. Simultaneous work-group sessions to inventory and report on knowledge and competencies needed by effective and innovative managers/executives.

    Project. Pretested self inventory of desirable knowledge and competencies.

2. The roles, responsibilities, tasks and required competencies of executives/managers as affected by different kinds of jurisdictions, functional fields, environments, and levels of responsibility.

    Project. Preparation of specifications covering responsibilities and qualifications for recruitment in filling selected executive posts.

    Alternate. Comparative analysis of roles and requisite competencies for different kinds of chief executive positions.

3. Characteristics of innovation, innovative managers, and means of creating innovative organizations.

    Project. Investigation of a recognized highly effective agency to determine the reasons for it; or contrast between an innovative and productive organization and one which is not.

    Alternate. Preparation of a plan by means of which a specified manager can keep abreast of new developments and technology relevant to his/her responsibilities.

4. Prevalent executive management deficiencies, breakdowns, and incompetencies; how to identify and cope with them.

    Project. Comparative evaluation of good and poor managers; available measures to convert poor managers into better ones.

    Alternate. Case involving optional methods for dealing with unsatisfactory performance of a manager.

5. Executive leadership, behavior, and individual change.

    Project. Matching perceptions others give of a participant's competencies and behavior with their own.

    Alternate. Management Appraisal Survey and Work Motivation Index.

6. Determining what treatises on management have most practical value.

    Project. Providing advice to an executive on the utility of a selected treatise on management in helping to cope.

    Alternate. Development of criteria for determining whether treatises and articles on management warrant reading and circulation.

7. Strengthening the administrative and innovative capability of governments, agencies, and enterprises.

Table 2.5 Continued.

Project. Evaluation of the administrative and innovative capabilities of a particular organization and how they can be increased.

Alternate. Development of workable methods for identifying and remedying administrative deficiencies.

8. Planning and creating organizations with high capability to achieve intended purposes.

   Project. Planning the establishment and organization of a state mandated Metropolitan Service Authority (MSA) or Mass Transit Agency (MTA).

   Alternate. Design of a new organization for agency X.

   Alternate. Application of organizational development (OD) principles to agency X.

9. Policies and methods for developing executive, managerial, and supervisory capabilities.

   Project. Mobilizing the managerial team for MSA or MTA.

   Alternate. Development and application of MSA's or MTA's personnel policy.

   Alternate. Installation of Likert's Management System 4 in MSA or MTA.

10. Strategies and instruments for defining, negotiating, and communicating, and securing support for objectives, policies, and programs.

    Project. Application of Management by Objectives (MBO) to MSA or MTA.

    Alternate. Preparation of a program budget for MSA or MTA.

    Alternate. Evaluation of agency X's planning, programming, budgeting, reporting practices, and preparation of recommendations for improvement.

11. Executive relations with legislative body.

    Project. Presentation of proposed program and budget to MSA's or MTA's Board.

    Alternate. Mock legislative hearing on budget of agency X.

12. Managing program operations to increase productivity and improve performance.

    Project. Developing a plan of operations and procedures for a selected MSA or MTA program.

    Alternate. Preparation of recommendation to improve performance of some agency program or service.

    Alternate. Evaluation of the administrative effectiveness of a selected program/service.

13. What an executive needs to know and do when appointed to a new post.

    Project. Taking over the directorship of MSA or MTA after a previous director is discharged for malfeasance.

Table 2.5   Continued.

Alternate. Taking over a managerial post in agency X.

Alternate. Development of a plan as head of a transition team for advising a new mayor, county executive, governor, comptroller general, enterprise manager, agency head.

14.   Executive use of managerial and other staff officers/units vis-à-vis line operations.

Project. Planning the various kinds and roles of staff units for MSA or MTA.

Alternate. Evaluation of the staff support arrangements in agency X and recommendations for improvement.

15.   Delegation and decentralization of program operations as requisites for dynamic, innovative organizations.

Project. Formulation and implementation of MSA's, or a state or federal agency's decentralization and delegation policy.

Alternate. Development of MSA's, MTA's, or agency X's policy in respect to fostering and rewarding innovative efforts.

Alternate. Analysis of delegation and decentralization in agency X and its effect on employee initiative and performance leading to proposals for change.

16.   The role of executives and managers in guiding institutional response to social, economic, and technological change.

Project. Response of MSA's and MTA's management to a major technological advance that outmodes its computer system.

Alternate. Response of MSA's management or that of a city to a 25 percent cutback in its budget resulting from a citizen referendum.

Alternate. Development of a program of "cutback management" for agency X.

17.   The values and ethics of public responsibility: coping with conflict of interest, kickbacks, bribery, political patronage, special privilege, and other diversion of resources.

Project. A prepared case study.

Alternate. Simulated problem in MSA, MTA, or agency X.

Alternate. Work group sessions to develop conclusions and proposals on some misfeasance featured in current headlines.

tions and less specially prepared background handouts could probably be produced for $30,000 to $40,000 depending on several factors outlined below.

The package would be prepared on 8½ × 11 paper and loose leaf in form, so that much of it can be extracted, edited, and reproduced by the instructor for participant use. The package might run from six to nine hundred single-spaced pages.

If a full-time professor with no or only partial reduction in salary were utilized as principal investigator, the amount of compensation could be lower. If an organization were used, charges would be much higher. The estimate assumes that a university could cover the salary for teaching the course for testing purposes but not the time for refinement of materials.

If a first-rate doctoral student or graduate assistant is available as the research assistant, the cost would be less than recruiting someone in the open market. Alternatively, a young coauthor drawn from a training center which has been experimenting with innovative material could be of enormous help. There has been some voluntary expression of interest in serving in this capacity.

It is desirable to include most of the background and reference material in the package. The question of permission for use of articles, chapters, and excerpts, from copyrighted publications is tricky. The less permission, the more original material must be prepared and the more reliance on reference materials on reserve for the course in the library.

Overhead is a major variable. Institutional support at the federally approved rate would add substantially to direct costs.

Income from Sales

An initial demonstration package should find four to six hundred purchasers. If sold for at least $50, the income should about cover costs of reproduction and marketing. A price of $75 to $100 would not appear unreasonable. However, funds available to professors for purchase of materials are often nonexistent.

Some subsidy for follow-up correspondence and assistance to users is desirable. Assuming that the purpose is to generate widest possible use, the charge should be enough to assure serious intentions by purchasers, but low enough to raise no barrier to purchasing.

Testing

Any budget for preparation of course packages should provide for pretesting. There would be no problem in getting five or ten institutions to use it and supply feedback. Inducements are necessary to secure prompt feedback reports. One is to charge $100 or so for the package and rebate the cost. The other is to provide an honorarium when critique is sent.

The author of the package should also test and revise material after each session in which he or she uses it. Several management development experts might also be asked to review it. Some executive training centers would gladly experiment with parts of the material. Many improvements will be made in this process.

Time

Six to nine months are estimated for the R&D and preparation of a preliminary edition, six months to pretest and secure feedback, and two months to prepare the copy for the first printed edition.

Market

An initial package of the type described should have a splendid market. An indication of the potential is shown by the success of the curriculum package on Intergovernmental Policy and Program Management. With very modest help from an IPA grant for reproduction and marketing, all 250 printed copies were sold in six months at $45 by the National Academy of Public Administration. Orders are still received, some from overseas although no effort was made to publicize it internationally. Education and training centers all over the world have the same need for materials.

The proposed generic package would serve a broad spectrum of potential users both in the United States and abroad. Interviews and correspondence with deans of graduate schools, heads of continuing education programs, individual professors, and directors of executive/management development centers revealed much interest and indicated that they would welcome the availability of packages. The most enthusiastic reactions came from executives in the U.S. Office of Personnel Management, Office of Management and Budget, and General Accounting Office, several federal departments, and state and local public interest groups. The following quotes from correspondence illustrate the general tenor of views.

Yes, this kind of material would be helpful to us and I hope NSF will assist this worthwhile project.

One great value of this effort would be to encourage faculty members to innovate. With the help of instructional packages they should be willing to venture to teach subject matter which they otherwise would stay away from because of their relative unfamiliarity with it and the time it would take to prepare themselves.

I would certainly support any effort to create more innovative courses in the managerial track, and would be delighted to work with you in that area.

Sometimes we in OPM begin to feel that we are the *only* ones who believe that there is an acute need in Government for better prepared managers. If indeed, it were possible to get NSF to fund preparation of course packages, it would be a great step forward.

Your proposed topics or modules are right on the mark. Not only would they challenge the learner's intellect, but also would offer practical experience in applying theory to situations.

Should the project come to fruition, we would certainly be a potential consumer (we consistently use your Intergovernmental Administration package). I would recommend to our faculty and to whoever else might listen that course work of this type be included in master's and doctoral programs which claim to prepare persons professionally for administrative, policy and program management responsibilities.

Any progress that NSF could make in helping to clarify the best means for teaching management skills, would certainly find a welcome market in the schools of public policy and public affairs.

One great advantage your proposed packages could offer would be . . . putting validity into university instruction. Your packages could force the pace in use of that which represents practical reality. . . . Second, I feel even more emphatic about use of the kind of packages you propose for inservice training and education.

Your appraisal of the Senior Executive Service and its potential for catalyzing efforts in public management education seems right on target. So, too, is your discussion of the need to develop curricular materials. . .particularly materials based on real life situations. Congratulations.

Managers do not have the most basic knowledge of management science, of management skills, and of specific management techniques to function as managers and make the administration of government work.

Any effort which NSF can apply in providing guidance and instructional material will be most welcome.

As you can imagine, I am extremely interested in working on the development of the package. At a very minimum, I could test the package in my MPA course.

Assuming that NSF is willing to commit considerable resources to its realization, it could make a valuable contribution to public management teaching. Some of our faculty would be inclined to try it out.

NOTES

1. Warren Bennis, *The Unconscious Conspiracy: Why Leaders Can't Lead* (New York: AMACOM, 1976), p. 145.
2. Graham T. Allison, Jr., *Public and Private Management: Are They Fundamentally Alike in All Unimportant Aspects?* Discussion Paper Series (Cambridge, Mass.: John Fitzgerald Kennedy School of Government, Harvard University, February 1980).
3. Selwyn W. Becker and Thomas L. Whisler, "The Innovative Organization: A Selective View of Current Theory and Research," *The Journal of Business,* Vol. 40, No. 4 (October 1976), pp. 462–469.
4. Chester Barnard, *Functions of the Executive* (Cambridge, Mass.: Harvard University Press, 1938).
5. Rensis Likert, *New Patterns of Management* (New York: McGraw-Hill, 1961).
6. Luther Gulick, *Papers on the Science of Administration* (New York: Institute of Public Administration, Columbia University, 1937).
7. Luther Gulick, *Administrative Reflections from World War II* (University: University of Alabama Press, 1948).
8. Barnard, *Functions of the Executive.*
9. I originally wrote "Tasks of Management" around 1946. Since then it has undergone extensive revisions for current use.
10. Laurie A. Broedling and Alan W. Lau, *Executive Summary: Navy Civilian Executive Study* (San Diego: Navy Personnel Research and Development Center, January 1979).
11. A summary of the full report, entitled "Transformation of Scientists and Engineers into Managers," can be found in James A. Bayton and Richard L. Chapman, "Making Managers of Scientists and Engineers," *The Bureaucrat,* Vol. 1, No. 4 (November 1972), pp. 407–425.
12. Henry Mintzberg, *The Nature of Managerial Work* (New York: Harper & Row, 1973).
13. This unpublished study, "Consolidated Compendium of Management Knowledge," was put together during the last two years by the Staff Development Branch of the Public Service Commission of Canada in Ottawa.
14. Donald C. Stone, *Professional Education in Public Works/Environmental Engineering and Administration: A Handbook for Establishing Centers and Programs* (Chicago/Washington, D.C.: American Public Works Association and the American Association of Schools of Public Affairs and Administration, 1974).
15. Thomas Mahoney, *Building the Executive Team: A Guide to Management Development* (Englewood Cliffs, N.J.: Prentice-Hall, 1961).
16. Rensis Likert and Jane Gibson Likert, *New Ways of Managing Conflict* (New York: McGraw-Hill, 1976).
17. Frank P. Sherwood's "Exploring the Nature of Executive Tasks and Responsibilities in the Federal Government" is a module in the Federal Executive Institute's "Executive Leadership and Management Program 1979," a three-week course given by the institute (Charlottesville, Va.).

18. Boedling and Lau, *Executive Summary: Navy Civilian Executive Study*.
19. David T. Stanley, *The Quality of Senior Management in Government in the United States*, A Working Paper for the National Academy of Public Administration (Washington, D.C., May 1979).
20. John A. Sussman, "Making It to the Top: A Career Profile of the Senior Executive," *Management Review*, Vol. 68, No. 7 (July 1979), pp. 15–21.
21. See, for example, Rensis Likert, *The Human Organization: Its Management and Value* (New York: McGraw-Hill, 1967), and many of Likert's other writings.
22. National Aeronautics and Space Administration, *Twelfth and Thirteenth Sessions—Management Education Program* (Washington, D.C.: NASA Management Education Center, 1979).
23. U.S. Department of Defense, *Defense Management Education and Training* (Washington, D.C.: U.S. Government Printing Office, August 1978).
24. Jennifer Lantrip, *Teaching Public Administration in the United States* (Richmond: Virginia Commonwealth University Center for Public Affairs, 1978).
25. James L. Sundquist, "Jimmy Carter as Public Administrator: An Appraisal at Mid-Term," *Public Administration Review*, Vol. 39, No. 1 (January–February 1979), pp. 3–11.
26. James L. Hayes, "Policy Statement on AMA's Plans for a Degree Program" (New York, January 30, 1980).
27. Advisory Commission on Intergovernmental Relations, *The Federal Role in the Federal System: A Crisis of Confidence and Competence* (Washington, D.C., July 1980).
28. Two documents define this need and outline content. See Donald C. Stone, *Guidelines for Developing a Master's Degree Specialization in Public Works Administration Within the MPA Degree* (Chicago/Washington, D.C.: American Public Works Association and the American Association of Schools of Public Affairs and Administration, 1979) and Stone, *Professional Education in Public Works/Environmental Engineering and Administration*.

Chapter 3

Notes For A "Public Management of Innovation" Curriculum

W. Henry Lambright

GENERAL ISSUES RELATING TO AN INNOVATION CURRICULUM

Need for Such a Curriculum

There is a need for an innovation curriculum. By innovation curriculum is meant an aggregation of courses systematically treating various aspects of the process of innovation in the public sector. Innovation refers to change in a general sense and of certain particular kinds, such as technological innovation. Public managers are increasingly involved in managing change—seeking some innovations, controlling other kinds of innovations, and assessing many for their utility in a particular context. Since they cannot avoid dealing with innovations produced by others, and must themselves engage—or decide not to engage—in innovative behavior, they should address more logically and objectively their capabilities to make better decisions with respect to innovation.

How do we know? There are performance gaps in public services that are obvious. These may be especially true in the case of urban services where problems are most severe and innovative solutions clearly needed. Energy and other resource-related issues require new technologies to be "innovated" if the American standard of living is not to plummet drastically. At the same time that there is a need to promote some kinds of innovations, there is an equal need to control other varieties more carefully. Three Mile Island, for example, suggests that nuclear technology is an innovation that has not been managed as well as it should have been. There are also a host of chemical hazards that have resulted in damages that might have been avoided with more attention to the regulation of these innovations.

Nature of need at different levels of government and within specific government levels. Each level of government has needs related to roles as promoters and controllers of innovation. The skills needed for promoting are different from those of controlling. Different agencies at each level tend to perform these contrasting tasks. Both promoters and controllers have to assess the need and risk of the innovation from their points of view.

Differences arise from where these promoters/controllers sit in the intergovernmental system. As a general rule, where scientific and technological innovation are concerned, the federal agencies play dominant roles related to development. They make the primary public decisions on which technologies are to be initiated and transferred. As regulators, they assess the new technologies for efficacy as well as for harm. Federal agencies play the key role at the front-end of technological innovation, especially as sponsors of basic research. Because of this role, public managers must deal with university grantees and high technology companies. They must link universities, industry, and federal laboratories. Also, they must relate programs to state and local sectors and industry through technology transfer and commercialization programs.

Local agencies are primarily users of innovations produced elsewhere. They must make intelligent choices as buyers of new technology and acquirers of innovations from outside the local system. In the process of using new technology and innovative practices, they must change. Innovation at the user side is just as demanding as at the production side.

States, standing in between, help or hinder federal producers/regulators, as well as local users. They are important especially in the incorporation by local users of novel practices and hardware. As middlemen, they can aid the federal agencies in adapting broad federal policy to local conditions. They can also help locals to gain the attention, assistance, and perhaps even funds from federal agencies.

The state is more than a broker or middleman, of course. It is a force in its own right, making policies for promoting and regulating change, and using innovations in the services over which it has control.

Types of students. We are concerned primarily with public administration students. While no effort should be made to exclude anyone, the goal is innovation in the public sector. This means students oriented to the public sector who select themselves by choosing to go to public affairs schools. The idea is to help them become more sophisticated with respect to their role in the process of change.

Probable Demand

Students, faculty, employers. There would be a reasonable demand on the part of students, faculty, and employers. By reasonable, I mean neither enormous nor trivial. There would be enough students within a typical public administration graduate program to justify a curriculum. If advertised to students outside of public administration, such as those in business administration or other professional schools, the number of students would increase. This should be done, of course.

With respect to faculty, the core professors should be drawn from public administration schools. However, there should be others from related fields. Linkages with business administration would be highly desirable, since industry supplies many innovations to the public sector.

Is there a demand from employers? Employers would be expected to be looking for people who are graduates of public administration schools, in general, as well as other professional schools. One would expect that students who begin from a good public administration base and who have taken an innovation curriculum also, would be perceived as standing out from the bulk of graduates. To the extent such a curriculum enhances their technological literacy, they will be even better off from an employer's standpoint.

Aside from traditional employers in public organizations, there are businesses with public sector orientations—such as aerospace industry contractors; and organizations such as utilities that are so regulated by the government that they could use some help in understanding their governmental environments. Graduates of an innovation curriculum who comprehend public sector buying behavior, as well as the government as a technological promoter or regulator, would be expected to be welcomed by corporations which must deal with government on a day-to-day basis.

Measurement of demand. How can we be sure there will be a demand? An answer is that we cannot be completely sure. However, we can look at analogous curriculum programs. There have been science and technology policy programs at various universities for a long time. The George Washington University program has been going strong for a decade. The theme has not been innovation per se. But, in being involved with science and technology, it has dealt with innovation. This program has always had a good and lively number of students. These students have generally had little trouble in getting jobs.

Harvard, Columbia, Cornell, and other universities have had programs of similar kinds. Whatever problems they may have had, student interest was certainly not one of them. The Syracuse University Maxwell School also has had a good experience with science and technology programs. It had one in the 1960s, backed by NASA money. The students associated with that program did quite well in being placed. More recently, Maxwell has initiated another program headed by me with a slightly different slant. This program has funds from the Sloan Foundation. It is much more attuned to innovation than was the first effort. This reflects my own concerns and interests. While the program is still relatively young, it can be said that the students who have chosen to relate to it have been quite good. Also, they have been able to get good jobs. We would hope that we could have about fifteen students a year in this program. While we call it a program, it is in reality an educational track or major within the general public administration curriculum. It might be mentioned that, in addition to the Maxwell School students, we also have been attracting a few others from different parts of the university, including some midcareer students.

So there is some evidence against which to measure demand. This evidence suggests an innovation curriculum just might work, especially if it gave some emphasis to public management of technology. This is an area where there are certain management skills that could be highlighted—technology transfer, technology assessment, for example. Technology transfer could be seen as an aspect of policy implementation; technology assessment, of policy analysis.

How do you stimulate? The best way to stimulate demand is to offer a decent product and then to get the word of its availability around. Getting to the students would be very important. It might be necessary to send out brochures to other universities making known the curriculum exists. Perhaps visits might be in order to these other campuses.

Of special importance is the quality of the first course that is taught under this curriculum. If the program is interdisciplinary, this first course might be taught by a team of professors. Such a showing of interdisciplinary participation would encourage student interest across disciplines.

It is important that the courses have a logical relation to one another. One might deal with the politics of innovation; another with the economics of innovation. There should also be a course that deals specifically with technological innovation and the issues surrounding it. A course to augment the student's technological literacy would also be desirable.

At the beginning of the school year, the faculty director of the innovation curriculum should speak with the public administration students about the offerings and why particular students might wish to consider a "major" in such a curriculum. As students get jobs in Washington agencies and other places, there would almost certainly develop networks and these linkages would provide an additional draw on students. Stimulating demand for this curriculum would best be done by the models provided by the graduates themselves as they move upward into positions of responsibility.

Once demand was stimulated one place, it could be further stimulated in other universities. Knowledge of the innovation curriculum at one university could be disseminated through meetings of professional associations such as the National Association of Schools of Public Affairs and Administration (NASPAA), and the American Society for Public Administration (ASPA). Materials used in the courses being taught by the initial adopters should be given out at these meetings and discussed.

Current Training in Public Management of Innovation

My understanding is that there are courses on innovation from the business side, an example of which is taught by Sam Doctors at the School of Business at the University of Pittsburgh. I understand that innovation curricula have been established at MIT and other universities with the aim of training new business entrepreneurs.

As noted, there are a host of science and technology policy courses and programs around the country. There have been successes and failures in the programs with which I am familiar. Generally, the failures have lain more with university politics than with the merit of the program. However, as pointed out, the market demand is likely to be good.

Transferability of Existing Activities

A very great deal is transferable. Much of the existing science and technology policy material is relevant. What is needed is a course that connects everything through emphasis on the process of innovation.

Such a course could also link the technology courses with those found in the typical public administration field dealing with organizational change.

This will require some adaptation. For example, it would not take much to get a course on "Policy Analysis" adapted to include a segment on "Technology Assessment." An "Organization Theory" course might be adapted to give more emphasis to organizational change. How this occurs depends on the individual professors involved. Whoever sets this curriculum up must be a skilled entrepreneur. How he gets it arranged will depend on what exists at the particular university at the time he moves.

Content of Curriculum

This program should deal with innovation in general, including organizational change. However, it would do well to give special attention to technological innovation. This would keep it from being too diffuse, since practically any course could be said to be in some way relevant to innovation. Technological innovation, however, would give a focus to the enterprise. It would not prevent discussion of other kinds of innovation, to be sure. If we look at it in this way, I would think a sequence of courses might appear as follows:

1. "Science, Technology, and Innovation" would be a very general introduction to the field in which these factors are considered to be monumental forces for change. They are forces that can work toward our benefit but can also cause harm. This course would begin with a discussion of technological innovation as an issue: examine good and evil perceptions of science, technology, and innovation. It would then go into the evolution of science and technology, indicating the mutual interactions between the two, and their relations to innovation. It would deal with contemporary issues, with particular emphasis on controversies surrounding certain technological changes, such as nuclear power. It would deal also, in a very broad way, with government structure and decision-making processes. The following literature would be relevant:

Huxley, *Brave New World*
Kuhn, *Structure of Scientific Revolutions*
Jungk, *Brighter Than a Thousand Suns*
Watson, *The Double Helix*
Greenberg, *Politics of Pure Science*
Lambright, *Governing Science and Technology*
Commoner, *Politics of Power*
Ames, *Outcome Uncertain*

2. A second course, "Public Management of Innovation," would have as its theme the interaction of government with innovation. While the bulk of the course would deal with activities at the federal level, it would also deal with the role of state and local governments as they relate to processes of science, technology, and innovation. One might use a particular area of current science and technology interest to illuminate key issues. Energy innovation could be selected. The course, or courses, relating to this subject would deal with all aspects—from atomic energy to conservation. However, the specific field would be merely for illustrative purposes. The aim of the course would be to provide general principles about institutional relationships, such as in promotional or regulatory modes. Some of the literature could include:

Rogers and Shoemaker, *Communications of Innovations*
Zaltman et al., *Innovations and Organizations*
Lambright, *Governing Science and Technology*
Lambright et al., *Technology Transfer to Cities: Processes of Choice at the Local Level*

Hans Landsberg, *Energy: The Next Twenty Years*
Sam H. Schurr et al., *Energy in America's Future: The Choices Before Us*

Stobaugh and Yergin (eds.), *Energy Future: Report of The Energy Project at the Harvard Business School*

In addition, use could be made of relevant items in such journals as *National Journal* and *Science*.

Course Strategy

The best strategy for teaching public management of innovation would be a combination of lecture/case study. However, there is a problem of relative absence of appropriate case study material. I think that this program is best fitted for master's-level graduate students. Innovation, particularly technological innovation, is a complex subject. It takes place in a variety of governmental and nongovernmental settings. In teaching public sector innovation, technological or otherwise, it is desirable to have students who already have some familiarity with these institutions, especially those of government.

With respect to the issue of theory/practice, the more theory the better. The problem is that we do not have much theory in the field of innovation. However, there are a few researchers, mainly who have worked under the aegis of Dave Roessner, and now J.D. Eveland, who have been trying to develop some more useful concepts about the processes of innovation. My "bureaucratic entrepreneur" notion is a case in point of the kind of concept that can guide research as well as the preparation of teaching materials for an innovation curriculum.

It would be helpful to involve individuals who have been identified by their professional peers as successful bureaucratic entrepreneurs. Such individuals could give guest lectures in the courses related to the innovation curriculum. Also, internships—getting students involved in practice—would be an equally useful way to proceed. If we could identify a few local bureaucratic entrepreneurs, we might assign selected students to work with these individuals and literally learn how entrepreneurs innovate through this technique of participant observation.

Time period. I do not believe it can be a viable curriculum unless it is at least two semesters. There are many public administration and public policy programs that are two years in length rather than one year—the latter being the length of the Maxwell School program. Such enterprises usually stress tools the first year and substantive policy specialties the second. Obviously, the longer the program, the more opportunity for establishing and giving depth to an innovation curriculum. "Innovation" is a cross-cutting theme—one that strengthens existing curriculum programs. It can also be a curriculum unto itself. If so, I would think it would need a distinctive flavor, and as I have argued, this could be supplied by the emphasis on management of technological innovation.

Students from different disciplines. Depending upon where the student comes from, he or she will have a particular bent. However, it should be a program that can appeal to a variety of different types of students. One variation might be an emphasis on federal policy. Another would be an emphasis on state and local policy. Still another would concern itself with business and regulatory issues. A curriculum that consciously sought linkages with business and law schools might want to lean in this latter direction.

SPECIALIZED ISSUES

My research has emphasized the critical role of local entrepreneurs and coalition-building in urban innovation. It suggests that in creating a network for innovation, attention must be given to the role of various actors necessary to make the innovation process move forward—or hold it up, when that policy is deemed appropriate.

If innovation is a process, then an innovation curriculum might well begin by recognizing this fact. It would seek to understand the dynamics of that process, the role proponents and regulators play in each stage, and how the curriculum might reflect the different kinds of information or skills needed at those different points in the process.

Innovative Awareness

Awareness is that capacity we would want in an innovator (bureaucratic entrepreneur) to look beyond his nose to the problems and/or opportunities just over the horizon. We would want him consciously to seek performance gaps now, and those that may be likely in the future. He would be sensitive both to present and long-range problems. He would have foresight.

It would follow from such a set of needs that we want to have in the curriculum both: (1) a futures orientation; and (2) an evaluative component—that is, the entrepreneur must constantly be critiquing his own program. These two ingredients seem somewhat incompatible but they are there. In the earliest stage, the entrepreneur must be aware of problems (he must evaluate) and opportunities (he must anticipate, have foresight and plan). He should have a measure of technological literacy, at least be able to read *Scientific American* in order to discern trends and new options in science and technology.

At the same time, the entrepreneur should be thoroughly familiar with the techniques of evaluation—how to produce a documentation plan, to look at an existing program as a national experiment, and to discern the gaps and issues. He should be able to separate genuine technological opportunities which might be pushed from technological white elephants which should be ignored. There are skills that can be taught in an innovation curriculum that will make the would-be entrepreneur more adept in the awareness stage.

Trigger

The trigger is an event, usually in the environment of the organization that catalyzes action—if there is an entrepreneur capable of taking advantage of the situation. Taking advantage implies a readiness to match an organizational need (innovation) with an environmental necessity (trigger).

What is involved is not so much that the entrepreneur have a ready solution as that he be able to react quickly to the environmental perturbation in a way that gets action started locally. He moves; he responds quickly to a "window" in the policy process.

Can this quick-response or timing capability be taught in any way? Awareness would seem a stage where analytic capabilities would be useful. Trigger is a stage where what would be needed is more a political timing sense. It may be possible to sensitize students to the need for timing in entrepreneurship. I would think that the best means for doing this would be case studies of successful and unsuccessful innovation experiences that illustrated timing—the uses of trigger—as a key variable.

Searching/Planning

This is a third phase, but it could occur earlier, depending upon the skills of the entrepreneur. The entrepreneur should be proactive, not reactive. He must be able to plan at front-end (awareness) so that when the trigger comes, he can be ready. Or he can do even more—help *create* the trigger by encouraging pressures from certain groups.

Encouraging pressures from certain groups is a delicate matter, since what the entrepreneur is doing often is getting outside allies to help him induce his own organizational colleagues to get moving. The danger is that in so doing, he will (1) alienate his inside colleagues; (2) be co-opted by the outsiders. All an innovation curriculum can do is make the entrepreneur sensitive to such possibilities and problems. Again, case studies can help on this political side of the entrepreneur's job.

However, wholly apart from these matters of who and how, there is an analytic side to the searching/planning function. What is at issue in these early stages of the decision-making process is governmental agenda setting. This activity can be totally haphazard or it can reflect a modicum not only of political accommodation (what is acceptable) but also policy desirability. The entrepreneur is taking issues from the system in general and placing them on the decision-making agenda of a particular institution. In doing so, he is selecting. This means the entrepreneur is, in effect, regulating or controlling certain innovations, keeping them off the agenda, or on the back burner.

Can searching/planning be taught? What kind of courses would be relevant? What kind of teaching materials would make sense? There must be a great deal of information available in a variety of sources. There are information retrieval systems galore and trained librarians to help obtain this information. But the searcher must know the right questions to ask and be thoroughly familiar with trade publications and general literature in a given field in which he wishes to innovate. He should be familiar with how to make the best uses of computer searches, because, increasingly, information of all kinds is being put on computer.

What is wanted is given more specificity during the search from which a limited set of options is selected. The actual decision is not made, but presumably the options are narrowed in accord with some criterion for selection. Such criteria should consist of a combination of the rational (what is the best solution to a given problem) and the political (what is acceptable). The innovator, no doubt, will "satisfice" under these conditions.

Planning, beyond search, but before adoption, implies putting flesh on the bones of a preferred solution or set of solutions. This means more specification. This is very difficult and calls for a mind-set more given to detail than that which engaged in long-range planning during awareness. At this point, the innovator is beginning to shape his solution or set of possible solutions to what he thinks will be feasible. He is planning; but he is also working on a proposal to advocate.

It would seem to me that this capacity to take broad ideas and narrow them gradually into proposal form (prioritizing) is a skill that can be taught. It is akin to development of an idea. While the idea itself may be a stroke of insight, if not genius, the taking of that idea and molding it into something practical is an activity that is amenable to training. It is public administration's equivalent of engineering development, once the basic invention has occurred.

Adoption

Adoption is the role we generally ascribe to elected officials. It is their job to authoritatively allocate resources on behalf of a political system—city, state, or nation. The innovation curriculum is aimed primarily in creating sophisticated bureaucratic entrepreneurs. We would expect that a percentage of such entrepreneurs would come from our public administration schools. The entrepreneur's skills here are an extension of those noted above—he must take his preferred solution or set of preferred options and market them to those who have the role to make decisions.

In training, we face the fact that in adoption, we are more in a political than rational/analytic realm. The entrepreneur must be able to speak and write cogently and persuasively. He must have some of the advocacy skills of the lawyer who musters as many facts as possible behind a position. Law students get training in advocacy through moot court processes. Public administration students need to have similar kinds of experiences. It matters little that they be aware, search, propose if they do not get their view adopted.

Innovation is a struggle for change. Students should arm themselves for the battle. Schools of public affairs should have courses and curriculum that provide mock exercises in program advocacy before groups of adopters. To make matters more realistic, they might place one group of entrepreneurs, favoring one solution, in competition with another group favoring a different solution—perhaps one that employs conventional technology. How would the advocate of something new cope with the arguments of those who have a technology that has been used for years? How could they deal with issues of financial, technical, and political risk? Students might be put into the various roles concerned with innovation—including one of trying to regulate or control, rather than push, a particular innovation.

Implementation

Implementation follows upon adoption. Once the political levels have legitimated, the entrepreneur must get the bureaucracy to go along. This involves yet still another set of skills, for the entrepreneur is now dealing with an organization. He may also be dealing with unions. He cannot assume complete agreement on the part of those charged with carrying out the innovation.

The entrepreneur would have to deal also with the clienteles of the agency whose practices he is trying to change. Strategies which are suitable for middle managers will have to be changed for employees. They will be different also with clienteles. Further complicating the implementation stage is the fact that the process of implementing may involve constructing facilities that involve novel features and this normal contractor procurement and management practices may not suffice. It is a fact that many state and local government procurement practices are inappropriate for implementation where demonstration projects are concerned. Therefore, training for implementation requires considering how to build novel arrangements within organizations and among organizations to get things done. It entails organizational design, procurement practices, and contractor management. It also may entail a heavy dose of personnel administration with the emphasis on union negotiations.

How many schools of public administration deal with such matters in an innovation context? Very few, we would expect. For years, implementation has been ignored in many academic writings even though it is in many respects the heart of public administration. Implementation involves art and political diplomacy. But it also entails organizational and administrative skills that can be honed and improved. The entrepreneur can learn better how to implement an innovation; to move it toward incorporation into the basic fabric of public service practices. But the curriculum materials to help him do so will have to be prepared.

Termination

Not all innovations work. In fact, we know that many barriers to innovation are desirable barriers because some innovations are downright harmful. Technology assessment at the selection stage, which takes account of risks, must be complemented by technology evaluation and monitoring throughout the innovation process. Risks and costs of technologies may show up during the implementation phase.

The aspiring public administration entrepreneur needs to be sensitized to the need to promote an innovation without being captured by the innovation. He must learn to recognize, as early as possible, problems with the innovation. When those problems are sufficiently grave and noncorrectable, he should initiate a termination process. Playing the regulatory or arresting role is not incompatible with that of promoting innovation. Terminating a particular innovation can aid innovation in general by saving money, energy, and administrative resources that can be diverted to a more worthy cause.

The entrepreneur turned terminator must terminate with a degree of sensitivity for the fact that not only he, but others in the organization (as well as supporters outside) have committed themselves to the innovation. People may have to be laid off or reassigned. Certainly, an innovation curriculum can address issues of equity and ethics in the termination process. Case studies probably are the only materials likely to highlight the processes by which termination can be carried out in ways that leave the organization receptive to second and third tries at innovation.

The innovation curriculum should begin by training the entrepreneur to be objective about the process of innovation. It does credit neither to him nor the institution that trained him if the entrepreneur has created a series of monuments that are Edsels by another name. Life does not begin or end with one innovation. The curriculum aims not at yielding *product* champions, but in creating individuals well-versed in the *process* of innovation. Such a curriculum, at least one focused on the public sector, probably does not exist at present. Some experiments aimed at seeing if one can be established ought to be tried.

POSSIBLE PLANS OF ACTION

Presume two levels of funding 1) $25,000 and 2) optimal. Let us assume that what is needed is an initial set of experiments testing the innovation curriculum. Those would probably take place in selected schools of public administration. They would use teaching materials prepared for testing as part of the experiment.

At the optimal level of funding—one not artificially restricted—we would recommend a test in at least three universities. In this optimal program several faculty members would be involved on each campus. New courses would be taught and novel teaching materials designed and written. The test of the innovation curriculum would run two years in each institution. At the end of the two year test, there would be an evaluation. The evaluation would extrapolate the best features of each of the three programs.

A serious effort would then be made, under a follow-on three-year grant to these same institutions, to apply the improved model to the programs underway at the initial three campuses where the best of the teaching materials would be used. Simultaneously, these three would be obligated to utilize channels in the public administration education community to disseminate the results of their experiences to other universities.

As part of this dissemination activity, an enlarged effort in developing case materials for an innovation curriculum to be used in many universities would be launched. Initially, this would be run by the original three universities. Eventually, if the innovation curriculum took hold and were institutionalized across the country, a larger consortium of universities could sponsor an ongoing effort in preparing and distributing case materials. The cost of this optimal three university, five year program would range from $500,000 to $750,000.

For $25,000, much less could be accomplished, but the concept could at least be taken off the ground. The best way to proceed would be to concentrate this money in one university already trying to develop a curriculum similar to the innovation effort we have contemplated. The funds would be used to strengthen this ongoing effort and influence its direction toward the innovation curriculum model.

Developing Detailed Curriculum

Under the optimal arrangement, each of the three universities would designate one individual at each campus as director of the innovation curriculum project who would be expected to work together as a committee to formulate general principles governing the innovation curriculum. They would coordinate on types of courses to be taught, special methods (such as interdisciplinary techniques), and materials to be used, and so forth. Each director would take responsibility to apply these general principles to the specific circumstances of his campus.

Under the $25,000 program, there could be only one campus and one director. He would develop the necessary policies and curricula. The funds could help in paying part of the salary of the director, freeing his time from work not related to the innovation curriculum effort, so that he could spend his teaching time on this project and develop a limited number of new teaching materials. At $25,000, the innovation curriculum could run one year.

Developing Necessary Training Materials

Under the optimal program, case writers and an editor would be hired to service the three universities. One university would take the lead on behalf of the three in managing the production function of the cases. However, the selection of cases would be up to the three universities as a group. Some of the funds would be used to commission cases from faculty members and graduate students.

Under the smaller program, the director or a part-time assistant would perform the role of writer/editor. The selection of the cases and their preparation would thus be in the hands of one university. Economies would derive from adapting existing cases, such as those we prepared in our Syracuse/Rochester project, for use in the innovation curriculum.

Identifying and Training the Trainers

Whether the program is large or small, the key to its success will lie in the ability and commitment of the participating faculty, and particularly the director. Identifying the leader and key faculty should be based on past performance. Those who have demonstrated interest and competence in innovation studies should lead this experimental effort. They can be expected to bring on new people from their campuses as necessary. The faculty who participate will learn by teaching. They will also learn by preparing, or supervising the preparation of case materials.

Testing Curriculum

In both programs, the test will lie in the manner and success of the curriculum's implementation. Either the curriculum will attract students or it will not. Either the students will like the innovation curriculum or they will not. Either the professors will feel satisfaction for what they do or they will not. Running the curriculum at one university one year will provide a minimal test. The larger program provides more time and opportunity for obtaining results as well as doing so in a way that is comparative.

Marketing Curriculum

Marketing would take place within the initial site or sites of the experiment. It would later take place from these early adopters to other universities.

Marketing within the university is difficult, but presumably the individuals chosen to lead the effort will have the necessary credentials and capacities to perform this task. Some memos advertising the curriculum to key advisers of students at the beginning of the year would be essential. It would also be helpful for the director to speak with the entering public administration students during their orientation session. Once underway, the curriculum would hopefully become better known through the student grapevine.

Marketing from the original test universities to other potential adopter universities will require the leaders of the program to perform an external role. They might well go to meetings of the National Association of Schools of Public Affairs and Administration (NASPAA) and American Society for Public Administration (ASPA). At those meetings, the leaders could take the opportunity to appear on panels.

At these panels, they could describe how the innovation curriculum had been received on their particular campuses. They could discuss its aspirations and initial results. Special reports could be prepared to be given out at these meetings. Also, the same kind of information could be put into brochures and these materials could be sent to universities throughout the country which have substantial public administration programs.

Assessing Impact of the Curriculum

The full impact of the curriculum would not be known for years. It would have to await graduates of the program obtaining jobs in government and then demonstrating substantial achievement. It would be useful to track the graduates of the innovation curriculum and, later, have them reflect on the merits of their training. Their employers could compare these people to others coming from the same universities who do not have innovation curriculum experience. Such methods might give some measure of the long-term effectiveness of the program. Until this becomes possible, impacts will be difficult to discern. This does not mean that evaluation will not take place. As indicated, it would take place throughout the implementation of the curriculum through the reactions of those participating in the experiment. Students, faculty, and the director will all have subjective reactions to what is taking place. The government would not be expected to provide a follow-on three-year grant in the larger test if it were not convinced that the initial two years were producing progress.

One measure of the success of the innovation curriculum will be the kinds of students who are attracted to it. Are these among the better public administration students at the university? Are the faculty who participate among the brighter and more imaginative people in the department? Are the jobs that the graduates get better than those non-curriculum students obtain? While the real assessment on the impact of the curriculum will take years to acquire, there will be short-term tests that will provide indicators of success or failure. One indicator will be the continuation of the program after federal money has gone.

Chapter 4

Curriculum Development for Public Management of Innovations: The Private Sector Connection

Samuel I. Doctors

GENERAL ISSUES

This chapter has three major purposes. The first is to assess the demand for, and availability of, academic and nonacademic education and training in the field of public management of innovations, and, more generally, the field of science and technology management by public sector administrators. The second is to discuss in detail the relevance of private sector management of innovation, in terms of both internal operations and new product development, to the public sector. The third and final purpose is to suggest a practical program for developing a curriculum for public management of innovations, and to describe how it could be tested in various academic and nonacademic settings to the advantage of students, training institutions, and the public sector at large.

In most state and local governments there is a dearth of technical knowledge and expertise in regard to modern technology and the methods of employing technology to increase productivity. The transfer and utilization of technology from the field of science and technology by state and local governments have been hindered by a variety of factors, of which the two most crucial have been: (1) that the professional training of most public sector managers provides little or no curriculum devoted to the managing or adoption of modern technology to the provision of public sector services; and (2) the lack of extensive private sector involvement in technology transfer and innovation adapted to public sector needs. It is essential that public administrators have the necessary skills in technology transfer, and that both public and private managers understand the mutual benefits of developing cooperative working arrangements in the development and application of new technology.

In order to assess the need for new and/or expanded curricula in the area of public management of innovation and, more generally, in the public management of science and technology, it is necessary to examine some of the different contributions of public officials at various levels of government to science and technology. The most expansive involvement by public sector officials in science and technology is by federal officials who, since World War II, have increasingly played a key role in almost all aspects of new technology development and, to a lesser extent, in its adaption and applications.

Federal officials in large measure have set the agenda and priority for technological development in direct support of research and development (more than 55 percent) as regulator, as supporter of science and technical education, and champion for innovation (Rickover, Mitchell, or Goddard, for instance) in market creation (for example, jet engines, helicopters, solid state electronics, and radar) and the transfer of innovation (the National Institute of Health, the National Aeronautic and Space Administration Technology Utilization Program, the National Science Foundation Intergovernmental Programs, and so forth). Thus any curriculum directed at federal officials must be concerned with preparing them for a variety of roles in the innovation process.

State and local officials have historically played a more limited role in science and technology, being mainly concerned with purchasing products that have already been developed and promoting their use within their respective agencies. Officials at this level have played only a limited role in direct support of R&D, in science and technology education, and in market creation for new products and services. However, through recently initiated intergovernmental science and technology programs, such as those shown in Table 4.1, it is hoped that state and local government can play an expanding role in science and technology as agenda setters and in market creation, both in terms of influencing federal agency policy and in creating a greater demand for more products and services with a greater science and technology (S&T) content.

Table 4.1   Federal Technology Transfer Programs To State and Local Governments

1. Urban Observatory
2. Pilot Cities Program (LEAA)
3. High-Impact Anti-Crime Program (LEAA)
4. National Institute of Law Enforcement and Criminal Justice—(LEAA) Technology Transfer Program
5. Federal Highway Administration—Implementation Division
6. California Four Cities Program
7. Urban Technology System
8. Totem I
9. Pilot States Dissemination Project (USOE)
10. Social and Rehabilitation Service Research Utilization Branch
11. Manpower Administration—Division of R & D Utilization
12. The New York City—Rand Institute
13. NASA—Technology Utilization Office
14. Integrated Municipal Information Systems Program (USAC)
15. Environmental Protection Agency—Technology Transfer Program
16. Urban Consortium for Technology Initiatives
17. Federal Laboratory Consortium
18. National Technical Information Service
19. National Science Foundation—State Executive Program
20. National Science Foundation—State Legislative Program
21. Innovations in Municipal Management (ICMA)
22. Project SHARE (HEW)
23. Office of State Technical Services
24. Innovations Transfer Project (CSG)
25. Smithsonian Science Foundation Exchange
26. TRISNET (DOT)

Source: Benjamin Gordon, *A Study to Review and Analyze Federal Efforts to Transfer Technology to State and Local Government,* report to the National Science Foundation (Columbus, Ohio: Battelle Laboratories, September 30, 1977), p. 14.

Frank Marini observes in *Science Leadership for Tomorrow* that "public administrators and policymakers at all levels of government most be trained and educated in ways that make them sensitive to the opportunities of technical developments and in ways that enable them to assess and to employ technological knowledge."[1] This need for management of innovations by public sector managers is dramatically substantiated by the passage of Proposition 13 and the tax-cutting and public expenditure-reducing initiatives it spawned. Over eighteen different tax and expenditure related measures appeared on the November 1978 ballot in states and counties across the nation with the intention of curtailing government spending. Commenting on what he terms the "year of the great taxpayer revolt," Robert Dworak points out:

The message from the taxpayer to the local government official is clear. There is a great deal of unhappiness with the property tax and with local government operations in general. . . . If for no other reason than the fact that the taxpayers expect it, local government officials should make every effort to increase the efficiency and effectiveness of their operations with a visible and strong concern for economy of operations.[2]

It is doubtful that this public attitude will result in a lowering of demand for delivery of public services, but clearly there is growing pressure for lower costs. The Gann's Initiative, colloquially known as the "Spirit of 13," which provided for expenditure limits on both state and local spending, passed easily in November 1979. State and local governments will have to try to maintain or increase the efficiency of services from existing resources and/or from shrinking revenues.

Public pressure for holding the line on public expenditure is both a threat to the status quo and an opportunity for innovative and creative public administration. It may be a threat if state and local governments adopt similar strategies to those used by many private sector firms during periods of budget pressure, that is, to cut new product development and promotion; it may be an opportunity, in that the efficient use of modern technology may allow government units to maintain or even improve the provision of services through increases in productivity during a period of downturn in revenues. The positive effect of measures such as Proposition 13 may indeed be the provision of an external stimulus for governments to increase their efficiency through the management of technological innovations. Such an external stimulus is often thought to be critical for motivating organizational change.[3]

A contradiction is evident in the public's desire to limit revenues while at the same time increase the demand for public services, and/or government action in such areas as transportation, social services, health care, and energy development. If government is to have any hope of reconciling these demands, it must innovate; to do so, the people it employs must be trained in the management of technological and other forms of innovation.

In May 1979, the American Society for Public Administration (ASPA) conducted a training needs survey of its 101 chapter presidents, representing over 16,000 members. Selected as the two highest priority topics for training were cutback management (managing with more limited resources) and productivity improvement.[4] This is an indication of both the need and demand for a curriculum devoted to the public management of innovations.

In 1977 J. David Roessner published a review of the body of recent research on the processes of innovation in state and local governments as part of an analysis of federal policies designed to stimulate the development, dissemination, adoption, and implementation of new products, systems, or managerial and analytic techniques by state and local governments. He concludes that federal policy should emphasize "strengthened analytic and evaluative capabilities of state and local government rather than the development and use of particular solutions—technologies, techniques and system."[5]

Roessner questions whether potentially successful technology transfer strategies are being hindered more by lack of demand on the part of users or by lack of supply of innovations, and concludes both are lacking and could benefit by improvements. With regard to demand, Wilemon's study of advanced technologies in five functional areas and their impact on the urban marketplace concludes that there is a general lack of a demand pull for new technology, except where the federal government has established a market.[6] Roessner's review of current research by Bingham, Yin, Feller and others, brings him to the conclusion that state and local agencies and those who work in them are not inherently resistant to innovation. They are, however, constrained by factors often not present in private firms which respond more directly to such stimuli as profit-increasing and efficiency criteria for innovation. Public sector officials and administrators often have to weigh short-term political time frames against a decision to implement technologies which may cost more in the short run but may achieve savings or efficiencies in the long run. The incentives promoting public sector managers to innovate tend to be different from those influencing private sector managers. An understanding of these differences is a critical preliminary step before incentives to innovate can be increased to any significant extent.

Roessner states, "The rate of technological change in government—the rate at which old or obsolete products and techniques are replaced by newer, improved versions—could be low if the rate of supply of innovations for the state and local government market is low, or if the innovations offered to this market do not match the pattern of demand."[7] He concludes, based on available research, that this is the case for at least some functional areas of state and local government services. The local government market is found to be highly fragmented, for example, in the fire service and law enforcement areas, making it unattractive to private sector investment in R&D and new product development. It is Roessner's opinion that "if the market were more attractive, it appears private manufacturers would respond with more aggresive marketing efforts, larger investments in R&D and a portfolio of projects more reponsive to the state and local market."[8]

Increased training in the management of technological innovation for public sector managers could enhance both the demand and the

supply sides of the technology transfer issue. Such training or education would build the capacity at the state and local levels for officials
"to define their problems in technical terms, identify alternatives that
may or may not include innovative solutions, and evaluate alternatives themselves or have the expertise to buy useful evaluative information from the outside."[9]

Public sector managers would be able to understand how technical
decisions can be interwoven with political realities and the need for
bureaucratic entrepreneurs as delineated in various studies conducted
by W. Henry Lambright.[10] They could better understand how the development of common technical specifications for products aggregate
markets sufficiently so that more private suppliers could enter the
public sector market, compete, and subsequently lower costs.

In short, the marriage of public sector demand and private sector
supply where both sides win, which has been a long time goal of technology transfer proponents, is realizable only if public managers are
familiar with the development and management of technological innovation from the private sector point of view, as well as from their own
self-interests. Conversely, there is also a need for private sector managers to learn more about the equity-oriented, bureaucratic survival
incentives that govern public sector performance and motives, which
often override or compete with motives to reduce costs, improve services or increase productivity. Private sector managers could then
capitalize on the potentially lucrative public sector market and also
appreciate how a more sophisticated public sector stands in the best
interests of the supplier.

Roessner suggests that, "ensuring that the latest accepted analytic methods and management techiques are part of the curricula of
the schools that produce public managers . . . should have salutary
effects on local officials' awareness and use of best available techniques and information."[11] He also believes that public interest
groups and professional associations could sponsor more continuing
education and training for their members and constituents in this
regard.

There is another side to this problem of awareness and understanding of the process of technological innovation, including technology
transfer—the need for more sensitivity by private sector managers interested in selling technology to the public sector. Private sector managers need training about the nature of public sector decision making
with regard to the process involved in the decision to seek out and
purchase some new type of technology, hardware or software. As mentioned previously, the constraints and time horizons of public sector
managers tend to be different than those facing private sector
managers.

From my experience in teaching private sector managers, it appears that graduate schools of business do very little to sensitize their students to the public sector market in general, and even less with regard to the public sector market for new technology. Thus, any suggestions for curriculum designed to train public sector managers to deal more effectively with the evaluation, purchase, and implementation of new technology must also consider the training needs of potential private sector managers who will be the principal means by which technology is sold to the public sector.

It is not within the scope of this paper to detail a curriculum for private sector managers. However, the general topic areas suggested below could be adapted for the use of private sector managers as could the attached syllabus, following in Appendix 4A, with some modest modifications. It is clear that the traditional emphasis in almost all graduate schools of business administration is on private sector economics, and thus provides little or no basis for understanding the public sector market. Generally, the only courses offered in business schools dealing with the public sector are those intended to train business students to cope with public sector regulation. This is hardly useful in understanding the public sector as a potential market for goods and services, particularly for innovations.

DEMAND

It is probable that the demand for a public management of innovations curriculum would be strong for at least three reasons:

1. The increasing complexity of government management resulting from:
   a. the enormous growth of services provided by the public sector in the past ten years, and
   b. the continuing increase in the numbers of state and local government employees and in overall spending.
2. The need to combat the decrease in confidence in traditional governmental management techniques, as shown by the recent passage of Proposition 13 and similar irate citizen denouncements of public spending of tax dollars in relation to public services provided.
3. The increase in the demand for public administration education focused on cutback management and productivity improvement, as expressed by the ASPA membership.

The ever increasing complexity of government management becomes evident when some data is even briefly considered. During the past twenty-five years, state and local government expenditures have grown at an unprecedented rate, about 856 percent in current dollars. The federal budget grew approximately 588 percent during the same time period.[12] In 1975 total expenditures by state and local governments were estimated at $265 billion, compared to about $28 billion in 1950. Part of the reason for the growth of the state and local government sector is the proliferation over the past ten years of federal grant programs which involve state and local governments. During the 1970s, Congress established approximately 150 new categorical aid programs bringing the total number to almost 500. Federal aid to state and local governments is running about $80 billion annually.

As the public sector grows, so does the number of persons it employs. Government service provided jobs for 15 million workers in 1976—one out of six employed persons in the United States. State or local governments (county, city, town, school district, or other special divisions) employed four out of five government workers; the rest worked for the federal government.[13] The Department of Labor has predicted that "continuing the trend begun in the late 1940s, employment in state and local government is expected to grow faster than the average for all industries through the mid-1980s."[14]

Despite the rapid growth in employment in state and local government, federal employment is expected to grow more slowly than the average for all industries through the mid-1980s. However, the proportion of federal workers employed in professional, technical, and administrative jobs has been increasing in recent years, while the proportion in clerical and blue-collar jobs has fallen. The Department of Labor expects this trend to continue. This attests to the increasing complexity of government service and to the potential demand for a public management of innovations curriculum from persons employed by the federal government.

In 1976, 750,000 state and local government workers could generally be found in governmental control and financial activities, including chief executives and their staffs, legislative representatives, and persons involved in administration of justice, tax enforcement and other financial activities and general administration. These categories included lawyers, judges and other court officials, city managers, property assessors, budget analysts, and clerks. The educational background of these kinds of jobs obviously would be law, business, or public administration. The Department of Labor predicts for the future that "a larger state and local work force also will be needed to provide improved public transportation systems, more urban planning and renewal programs, increased police protection, better measures to guard against air and water pollution, and expanded natural resource

Table 4.2   Growth in Separate Departments of Public Affairs/Administration[a]

	Numbers of Programs			
	1973	1975	1977	% of Change
Separate professional school of PA/A (i.e., reports directly to central university administration in the same or similar manner as a law school)	25	29	32	10%
Separate department of PA/A in large unit (such as a social science division, college of arts and sciences, etc.)	23	35	49	40%
Professional school of PA/A combined with another professional school (e.g., business school)	11	8	5	-38%
Department of PA/A combined with another department (e.g., business administration)	6	14	8	-43%
PA/A program within a political science department	36	52	62	19%
Total	101	138	156	13%

Source: Reproduced with permission from National Association of Schools of Public Affairs and Administration, *Programs in Public Affairs and Administration,* 1978 Directory, Washington, D.C. 1978.
[a]Undergraduate programs are not included in this table.

development programs."[15] All of these activities have technological components.

Of the 396,000 lawyers working in 1976, 29,000 worked for the federal government and 41,000 for state and local governments. Sixteen thousand urban planners were employed in 1976. Most of these jobs required two years graduate study in urban planning. In 1976, 3,000 city managers were employed. In addition, approximately 9,000 persons worked as administrative assistants, department head assistants and assistant city managers.

In 1973, 101 colleges and universities offered graduate degree programs in public or municipal administration; in 1976 the number increased to 156 (see Table 4.2). An MPA or MBA has become an essential qualification for city manager positions. The Department of Labor predicts that "employment of city managers and local government management assistants is expected to expand faster than the average for all occupations through the mid-1980s as management of our governments becomes more complex."[16]

The Department of Labor states that the council-manager form of government is the fastest growing form of city government. This will only intensify the demand for trained city managers and management assistants in the future.

If the growth of academic offerings can be considered as a response to a demand, then the demand for public administration instruction has been increasing very rapidly. As indicated in Table 4.2 since 1973 there has been significant growth in separate academic departments of public affairs/public administration. A 1977 survey conducted by the National Association of Schools of Public Affairs and Administration (NASPAA) shows that during the 1976–77 school years, of the 156 institutions offering graduate degrees:[17]

106 offered the MPA
50 offered the MA
17 offered the MS
7 offered the MUA
38 offered the PhD
9 offered the DPA
48 offered some other graduate degree such as the MAIS or MA/CJ.
(The total exceeds 156 because some institutions offer a combination of degrees.)

However, this proliferation of programs in the public and municipal administration field does not indicate the extent of innovation management available in the area, a need which the 1979 ASPA made clear.

With regard to the total numbers of graduate students involved in this type of education, 7,990 full-time students were reported by 146 programs, with full-time being defined as enrollment in three or more courses per academic term; 16,486 part-time students were reported by 147 programs. This means a total of 24,836 full-time and part-time graduate students were enrolled. Increases in enrollment of part-time students accounted greatly for the growth in enrollment, as well as the fact that eighteen more programs were reported in 1977 than in 1975.[18] In 1977 the total number of graduate degrees awarded was 6,616 compared with 4,407 in 1975. In 1977, 5,075 MPAs were awarded and 929 MAs or MSs were awarded.[19]

THE RELEVANCE OF THE PRIVATE SECTOR TO PUBLIC MANAGEMENT OF INNOVATION

To meet taxpayer demands for adequate or better services with constant or decreasing levels of revenue, state and local governments need to increase their productivity. Technological innovation offers a way to increase productivity through the introduction of new products or hardware and/or the introduction of new management techniques, systems analysis, and so forth.

Likewise, the need for private sector involvement in the transfer and utilization of technology should be encouraged. The small, high-technology company, in particular, is critical in the development, transfer and adaptation of important new technology. This is because smaller businesses (as opposed to larger companies) have the flexibility and adaptability to deal effectively with the complex, fragmented market that is state and local government.

In the last decade, there have been a number of federal capacity-building experiments which have attempted to improve the efficiency and effectiveness of state and local governments through the transfer of technology. These have included NASA's Technology Utilization Program, the National Science Foundation's Intergovernmental Programs, including the Urban Technology System and various regional innovation groups in New England, the Pacific Northwest and elsewhere, and the Federal Laboratory Consortium. Thus far, these programs have been unable to deal adequately and/or effectively with inducing a high level of private sector involvement in their activities. More dollars need to be made available by federal mission agencies to private sector firms, and sufficient market aggregation will have to be induced in selected areas to motivate private firm R&D spending to impact on these efforts.

The private sector management of innovation intersects with public sector management of innovation in two key areas: market development and technology transfer. Two important questions arise in these areas: (1) In terms of a state and local market for new private sector products, what are the market's characteristics and what does that mean for suppliers? (2) In terms of processes, how does the selection, adoption and diffusion of technologies in state and local agencies differ from those processes in the private sector? For example, one area of commonality identified is the need for an entrepreneurial function in both.

There is a need for public sector managers to better understand the management of innovations from a private sector point of view. They need to understand more about the unique features of private sector firms which produce and sell technological innovations as well as the economic benefits from their communities that can be derived as a result of the financial success of such firms. For example, there is evidence that the growth of smaller advanced technology firms in the Route 128 area near Boston which have significant technology transfer capabilities, has improved substantially the economic climate of that geographical area, and to some degree has begun to reverse the economic decline prevalent so long in the New England area.[20]

The private sector manager needs to gain a better understanding of the factors (both positive and negative) which influence the demand for new equipment/processes. Also, the private sector manager needs specific training and experience in the transfer and application of technology in the local government context.

Richard Rosenbloom points out that one of the main reasons for problems of productivity improvement in the public sector is that it lacks the infrastructure for innovation adoption and use. He recommends that in order to improve productivity, governments must learn to make better use of modern management techniques, and more technically trained people must be employed in the public sector. Most important, from the standpoint of this chapter, is Rosenbloom's observation that productivity could be improved if businesses which supply goods and services to government would encourage the use of more productive technology and systems.[21]

The private sector is better equipped than the federal government to supply technology because of its inherently greater flexibility to meet customers' needs and to adopt technology for a wide variety of applications. The private sector is experienced in adopting technically sophisticated goods and services to individual user needs. Finally, most technology is produced by the private sector. While the federal government sponsors or contracts for more than 50 percent of all R&D, the private sector is still the primary actor in the R&D process because more than 85 percent of all R&D is performed by private sector firms.[22]

What conditions would prompt the private sector to become more interested in stimulating local government innovation? Certainly, one such condition would be more aggregation of the state and local government market and an increase in its potential to purchase new products resulting from private sector R&D.

The state and local government market consists of over 79,000 decision-making units, including more than 19,000 municipalities, 17,000 towns, and 15,000 school districts. These in turn consist of functional departments which often control purchasing decisions, and differ radically in their perceptions of needs.

Roessner, in his study, "The Local Government Market as a Stimulus to Industrial Innovation," posits four conditions that influence a firm to invest in research and new product development:

1. market size sufficient to promise an acceptable return on investment;

2. market aggregation sufficient to promise economies resulting from volume and to keep market costs to an acceptable level;
3. willingness of the market to accept new or improved products; and
4. an industry structure, tradition and economic condition conducive to investment in R&D.[23]

The fragmented market problem is accompanied by other characteristics of public organizations which hinder decisions to innovate at the state and local government levels. As Roessner points out, public organizations, unlike private ones, lack a high degree of control by top executives due to the existence of multiple appeal routes to external organizations. Thus, the uncertainties associated with innovation are less likely to be tolerated by organization members or heterogeneous client groups.[24]

Public sector organizations lack the profit motive which promotes more efficiency, and they are constrained in their ability to shift or reduce personnel to modify operations as conditions change. Municipal purchasing and procurement practices hinder innovations by making the low bid the controlling criterion in the selection of equipment. Innovative design, low maintenance, or long-term durability are not taken into account in the decision to purchase. Finally, public sector personnel are often unable to describe their problems or needs in technical or economic terms that private firms can respond to or understand in terms of future marketing potential.

The federal government could help create conditions which would lead to more private sector participation in state and local government technological innovation. Roessner confirms the thesis of this chapter when he states that federal strategies should include "the support of training programs and curriculum development to enhance the technical and managerial capabilities of present and future city officials." He believes that "the most promising leverage point for federal policy intended to increase technological change in municipal services concerns local government's ability to identify problems systematically and define them in technical terms, to search for alternative solutions that include but are not restricted to innovative ones, and to evaluate the alternatives."[25]

The federal government could provide subsidies for performance contracting to state and local governments to replace low bid contracting where appropriate. Some of the experience of the Department of Commerce's Experimental Technology Incentives Program (ETIP) could be used in the design of this effort. Federal subsidies could be developed for state and local governments which would provide sufficient overhead funding to private sector firms performing development work for state and local governments. This would enable them to fund overhead R&D costs in a similar fashion to what is now done under federal R&D contracts and has become a crucial element in the development, by private firms, of new, high technology products and/or services for their federal customers.

Roessner's research of technological change in four functional areas of local government service delivery—fire protection, law enforcement, urban mass transit, and wastewater treatment—concludes that federal intervention strategies to increase innovation "will literally have to be tailored to each functional area of concern."[26] He suggests that in the fire services, the federal government might take advantage of the apparent success of new entrants in the supplier industry. It could encourage market entry by providing market information and analyses or by engaging in cooperative marketing or demonstration efforts. Because law enforcement innovations tend to be spinoffs from a firm's investment in R&D for another market, Roessner suggests that the federal government could increase communication between law enforcement officials and prospective manufacturers. For the mass transit industry, he suggests that the introduction of federal performance-related standards might enhance the attractiveness of the market for manufacturers.

Since smaller entrepreneurial firms tend to innovate at higher rates than do larger organizations, a 1978 Office of Technology Assessment report suggests that Congress should take action to ease the problem of entry for new firms as well as improve chances for their survival against stronger, more established firms. Such actions might include early venture capital assistance; selective use of government procurement to assist new technologically innovative firms; stricter antitrust enforcement; consulting assistance to new firms in meeting regulatory requirements; and more favorable tax treatment for new firms (for example, longer carry-forward provisions and changed depreciation-lower capital gains tax).[27]

Irwin Feller, Donald Menzel, and Lee Ann Kozak contend that the impact of a system of federal certification (of technical capability) on the rate of technological diffusion is complex and difficult to evaluate.[28] They believe that the appeal of certification to private manufacturers is "inversely related to (a) their established position within a functional area, and (b) their size." Firms seeking to enter the public market and/or smaller firms are more likely to favor public sector certification which underwrites part of the marketing expenses such firms would otherwise incur. Firms already in these markets are more likely to prefer an informal system of technical certification based on a company's reputation. They conclude, "In this respect, federal decisions toward technological innovation may affect the competitive positions of new and established firms."[29]

The process of innovation in the private sector begins with a new scientific theory, discovery or invention which proceeds through a number of trials and experiments, market probes and tests, laboratory models and production models, until the concept is reduced to practice as a profitable new product, process and/or service. This overall process may take many decades, as in the case of radio or atomic energy, or a somewhat shorter period, as in the case of xerography or solid state electronics. There are two divergent conceptual frameworks that explain the process: the more popular and widely accepted "rational" view of Burton Klein,[30] James Bright,[31] James Bryan Quinn,[32] and most economists; and, the less "rational" view of Donald Schon,[33] and James March and Herbert Simon.[34] Public sector managers who wish to manage the evaluation, purchase, and adaptation of new technology need to have some understanding of this total process as well as an appreciation for the implications of the two divergent concepts that seek to explain the process if they are to do more than simply react to the "hawking" of private sector vendors or to federal grant programs. This understanding will require both an academic base and job experience in managing technological innovations.

The views expressed by Schon and by March and Simon emphasize the importance of outside pressures of one kind or another on the decision to accept new technology. The rational view emphasizes the identification of needs, the evaluation of alternatives to meet those needs, and the decision to purchase the optimal alternative technology to satisfy the needs. However, there is evidence that more important to adoption decision, at least in some instances, is a dissatisfaction with the existing system because of outside intervention, a kind of "technology push" situation. Thus, programs of technology transfer that proceed solely on the rational needs assessment basis are not likely to be as successful as a more mixed strategy might be. Training programs for public sector managers must recognize the need to provide curricular experiences which explore both views of the adoption process and indicate the managerial implication of each.

One area of great importance is the recent research on the innovation process in both public and private organizations which identify entrepreneurs, risk takers, and "champions for innovation" as critical to the innovation process. On the private sector side, studies by Colin Gilfillan, David McClelland, Ed Roberts, Donald Schon, and Daniel Shimshoni are noteworthy.[35]

Roberts' study of the new advanced technology firms in the Boston area reveals that "the movement of technical personnel, namely the technical entrepreneurs who initiated these businesses, were found to be the critical element in transferring technology across organizational lines."[36] Shimshoni studied the growth of the scientific instrument industry after World War II and found that "technical entrepreneurship accelerates the process of innovation" and that "technical personnel are the key element in transfer."[37] Schon's research on the adoption of new ideas in large organizations identified the need for new product champions.[38]

On the public sector side, Lambright's research identifies a parallel need for internal entrepreneurs in the adoption of innovations in local government. He states, "The key factor in urban government innovation is the local entrepreneur. Under most conditions, this is a bureaucratic entrepreneur."[39] Public sector entrepreneurs, as Lambright conceptualizes them, "contribute the push that builds local demand."

> Entrepreneurs can be adopters, implementers, suppliers, or clients. As entrepreneurs. . .they form links among the other local actors as well as between local government and external organizations such as state and federal governments. They may or may not be product champions in the traditional sense of the innovation literature. The essence of their skill is problemsolving in a technical and political context. The entrepreneur. . .links problems with technical solutions and then pulls together groups necessary to complete an innovation process.[40]

Lambright suggests that "local entrepreneurs need to be strengthened in terms of both their technical and political capacities," and "new training materials might well be sponsored that would create a new generation of local officials who better combine these skills."[41]

The concept of technical entrepreneurship cannot be overstressed. As a method of transfer of technology from one institutional setting to another, it has proven to be the most successful vehicle yet found. It relates to both the supply and the recipient sides in state and local government technology utilization in that private sector entrepreneurs are a key element in identifying and adapting new technology for public use and the public sector entrepreneur is critical for selling the new ideas internally.

Although it is unlikely that one can develop either private sector or public sector entrepreneurs through any type of academic training program, it is important that we recognize them as the critical element in the overall innovation process, including the transfer process. This recognition should take the form of identifying such individuals and helping their development by providing skill training. Also, organizations can be structured to provide a more welcome environment for them. In addition, other persons are important for the innovation and attendant transfer process. Such individuals include those identified as "cosmopolitans" and/or "gatekeepers." These people provide important information channels for diffusing information about new technology. Here we find that trade associations, professional associations, and other information networks may be important to provide additional access points for the private sector and public sector cosmopolitans and gatekeepers.

Also, both private and public sector managers need to be trained to better encourage and utilize entrepreneurs and cosmopolitan gatekeepers. The improved management of these individuals may include allowing for more scope of operation and more freedom to develop their ideas even if they seem initially less orthodox.

This problem or organizational structure to encourage innovation is a very complex subject, and there is no intent in this brief discussion to do more than indicate that any training program aimed at increasing the acceptance of more innovation in the public sector will have to be directed at a variety of individuals holding different positions in both private and public sector organizations.

POSSIBLE PLANS OF ACTION

The simplest plan of action to implement would be to introduce a course in graduate schools of public and business administration and law schools which would help the students to become more innovative managers. In addition to planning such a course designed for these separate schools, it would be valuable to set up an interdisciplinary course which would bring together instructors and graduate students from different academic backgrounds such as business, law, public administration, and other fields. Bringing together these people from diverse backgrounds would promote lively discussions and valuable insights from the participants' various perspectives.

Whether the course be limited to particular schools or interdisciplinary in nature, it should cover the following topics as a minimum:

Process of technological innovation
Policy issues for management of the innovation process, including technology transfer
Federal government policies and their effects on innovation
Legal/regulatory issues in innovation
Technical entrepreneurship and the gatekeeper function
Organizing to promote the introduction and adoption of more innovation

The private sector milieu for innovation versus the public sector milieu for innovation

Forecasting technological change and the need for such change

A syllabus, which might serve the purpose with some small adjustments, is appended as Appendix 4A. The course represented by this syllabus has been taught at three different universities during the past twelve years. Although most of the students were graduate students in the school of business administration, graduate students from schools of public administration and law have often participated. One problem for the pedagogy of such a course is the dearth of more recent teaching materials such as case studies. Some attention should be paid to the development of more recent case studies and related readings.

Another important problem with offering a new course in an academic setting is obtaining approval from the requisite academic committees and finding faculty members who are motivated and qualified to teach such a course. This is not simple since new course offerings in most schools require a complex approval process and qualified, motivated professors are not in large supply. This type of course could probably be offered at a few schools for several years with some modest support from the National Science Foundation. This would provide time to produce course development, and to bring four or five professors together occasionally to compare their classroom experiences, thus enabling them to write a final report which could be presented at various academic meetings.

Three more plans of action are set forth below. The first represents a minimum effort through which a basic curriculum package could be developed and a limited amount of testing would take place. The second represents a full scale effort which includes the development of practitioner and academic training programs and their testing in a variety of different institutions with evaluation of the results. The third plan includes a research component. All three cases involve development of these core courses: "Public Management of Innovation—Organizational Dynamics," "Private Sector Role in Public Management of Innovations," and "Technology Transfer."

As I discussed earlier, there are a variety of ongoing educational efforts related to the public management of innovations currently being conducted. None of these adequately addresses the actual question of the management of public innovations, and none specifically zeroes in on the role of the private sector. Ideally, intervention to add such components would occur in three sectors: selected academic institutions, that is, schools of public administration, law, business and engineering; public interest group training efforts; and federal government training efforts. In addition, ideally, a complementary research program would be conducted to fill certain existing data gaps important to the success of carrying out these proposed plans of action. Finally, two long-range ultimate goals might be sought: the institutionalization of a minor in public management of innovations in any or all of the academic institutions mentioned above, and/or the development of a mobility program through which public sector and private sector managers could serve on temporary assignments on the other side of the fence.

Plan 1

This envisions a six-month effort which would include:

1. Development of a core course in public management of science and technology-based innovations based on private sector roles, relationships, and operations. This would include a complete course package, including specific case studies, literature to be assigned, outcomes to be achieved, identification of a faculty team to teach the course including one academician, one private sector individual from an organization such as the General Motors Institute, and one private or public sector practitioner.
2. Contacting the institutions with the eighteen programs listed in Appendix 4B, Note 1 in order to ascertain the current content of their science and technology courses and determine what incentives they would need to incorporate a curriculum such as that outlined in this chapter.
3. Contacting both the ICMA Training Institute and ASPA Training Institute to ascertain their interest in the incorporation of such a course.
4. Contacting the Office of Personnel Management to ascertain its interest in the incorporation of such a course.
5. Preparation of a detailed curriculum to include the course above, plus suggested courses in the functional areas of administration (budget, personnel organization development) which might accompany it in a school of public administration, business administration, law or engineering.
6. Development of a list of all the candidate institutions—public, private, nonprofit—to which the core course package could be marketed.
7. Development of a proposal to test the curriculum package in selected various institutions (see Plan 2 below).
8. Development of a short paper on criteria for assessing the impact of such a curriculum, including both short and long range im-

pacts on students, institutions using the curriculum, and the public and private sectors generally.

The above eight tasks could be accomplished for less than $25,000 over a six-month period. It is anticipated that at the end of this period a program would be completely ready for testing; the institutions where it would be tested will have taken the necessary steps to accept this package on a test basis; and faculty will have agreed to participate. All that would be necessary would be the approval and funding of the testing proposal to start a one-year testing program.

Plan 2

This envisions an eighteen-month, two-year effort at an optimal level of funding of between $100-200,000 depending on how many institutions are involved. It includes all tasks of Plan 1 above, and administrative costs for the one-year testing program.

As part of Plan 2, four to six academic institutions would be identified and the public management of innovations curriculum package would be tested, including teaching the core courses for one semester. In addition, there would be testing of a different format of the curriculum package. It would be developed into an intensive three-day (Friday, Saturday, and Sunday) or five consecutive (three-hour) evening seminars. This would be designed for administrators already working in local, state, or federal government and would be tested under the auspices of a public interest group, ASPA, and/or the Office of Personnel Management. In all cases, it is anticipated that some amount of funding would be provided for participating institutions. The amount would be determined as part of the activities in Plan 1 which constitutes the first part of carrying out Plan 2.

Plan 2 anticipates monitoring the testing efforts at the various institutions. Evaluation will be discussed in a comprehensive report on the results of the testing efforts which would compare outcomes based on the different types of institutions involved and which recommends a future course of action.

Plan 3

Plan 3 incorporates all of Plans 1 and 2, but includes a research element designed to fill data gaps relative to the effective involvement of the private sector in technology transfer and utilization by state and local governments. These include the following:

1. Research on how state and local governments classify and report data on their expenditures in order to determine what amount of

the expenditures are simply committed costs and how much are discretionary and could be used to purchase new technology. This would help identify the real leverage points in state and local government spending that might be used to induce greater use of modern technology.

2. Development of a data base which identifies the characteristics of businesses providing goods and services to the state and local government markets, including their size distribution, business specializations, relative capital intensity, the extent they have acted as technology transfer agents or technology adopters, and the effects of federal grant programs and federal regulations on their behavior with respect to the state and local market over the past ten years.

3. Research on the behavior patterns of state and local government that may affect technology transfer and utilization due to power shifts resulting from federal court decisions such as Baker vs. Carr.

4. Research on technical entrepreneurship and the role of small, high technology companies in the transfer of technology across institutional lines.

5. Research on the nonadoption process at the local or state level, both where such decisions lead to positive organizational results and where they lead to negative or less than optimal results.

Practical Programs

As has been shown in the preceding discussion of available training programs, few existing efforts are targeted directly to the public management of innovation. There are, however, many courses offered that are complementary to a public management of innovations course of study. The issue then becomes not so much what is transferable, but rather what can be added to existing efforts so that an overall education in a discipline such as public administration, business administration, law, or engineering, could be enhanced by a public management of innovations component.

Content of Curriculum—An Example

A Public Management of Innovations curriculum should be graduate level. The envisioned curriculum for academic institutions would result in the equivalent of a minor in conjunction with a principal area of study in one of the following: public administration, business administration, law, or engineering. That is to say, students would pursue basic required courses in these areas, but in addition they would also take three required courses and select two electives which would enable them to achieve the equivalent of a minor in Public Management of Innovations. For example, an MPA candidate would take basic administration courses such as personnel, financial management, and quantitative analysis, as well as the three required courses and a minimum of two electives which satisfy both MPA and Public Management of Innovations minor requirements.

Outline of Content

1. Basic Required Courses in Public Administration, Business Administration, Law or Engineering
2. Required Public Management of Innovation Courses
   a. Public Management of Innovations—Organizational Dynamics
   b. Private Sector Involvement in Public Management of Innovations
   c. Technology Transfer
3. Possible Electives[42]
   a. Organizational Development/Organizational Change
   b. Law and Technology
   c. Intergovernmental Relations
   d. Technological Forecasting/Assessment
   e. Urban Technology
   f. International Technology Diffusion
   g. R&D Management
   h. Science, Technology and Public Policy
   i. Productivity Improvement
   j. Systems Analysis

In the required courses, a case study/lecture format would be used. Both theory and practice would be emphasized.

In addition to an academic institution curriculum as outlined above, it is believed that the three required courses could be adapted into a three day seminar for practitioners.

The objectives of the Public Management of Innovations curriculum are to provide understanding of and familiarity with:

The history of public management of innovations, including federal policy and programmatic initiatives

R&D efforts nationwide: federally sponsored, private, and federal laboratories

Key concepts: innovation, technology transfer, entrepreneurship, research, applied research, capacity building, and technology agents

Private sector roles and contributions, product development, venture capital, and return on investment

Public versus private organizations: barriers to innovation, "innovativeness," and the nature of decision making in each

Innovation development process, the adoption process from idea to commercialization

Productivity improvement, new technology approaches versus participative management approaches

Market and purchasing, aggregating markets, purchasing, and procurement

R&D management

Some Key Literature

March and Simon, *Organizations*

Rogers and Shoemaker, *Communication of Innovation*

Annual Reports of the National Commission on Productivity

Hayes and Rasmussen, *Centers for Innovation in the States and Cities*

NSF-sponsored papers/reports of the last five years by Roessner, Feller, Doctors, Yin, Lambright, Bingham, and Rogers

Reports of the U.S. Congress Committee on Science and Technology, Subcommittee on Science, Research and Technology

Blair, *Industry, Innovation and the Municipal Market*

Gruber and Marquis, *Factors in the Transfer of Technology*

Gilfillan, *The Sociology of Inventions*

Schmookler, *Invention and Economic Growth*

Cooper, *The Funding of Technologically Based Firms*

Shimshoni, *Aspects of Scientific Entrepreneurship*

Schon, *Technology and Change*

Bright, *Research Development and Technological Innovations* and *Technological Forecasting for Industry and Government*

Urban Institute, *The Struggle to Bring Technology to the Cities*

National Science Foundation, *Technology and the Cities*

Eveland, Rogers, and Klepper, *The Innovation Process in Public Organizations*

Allison, *The R&D Game: Technical Men, Technical Managers, and Research Productivity*

Cetron, *Technological Forecasting*

Gerstenfeld, *Effective Management of R&D*

Jewkes, Sawers, and Stillerman, *The Sources of Invention*

Mansfield, *The Economics of Technological Change* and *Industrial Research and Technological Innovation*

Morton, *Organizing for Innovation: A Systems Approach to Technical Management*

Price, *The Scientific Estate*

Conclusion

There is a need for more and better training in science and technology for state and local government officials, but there is also a concurrent need for training for private sector managers who expect to sell technology to the public sector. Both need training in the process of innovation including the problems of transferring technology across institutional lines.

Of course, with such training and education programs confined to a single school or discipline, it may not be as successful as might be wished. Using the interdisciplinary seminar taught at the Kennedy School of Government (Science and Public Policy, but geared to the state and local level) as a model, we might try to develop a seminar that brings together graduate students and practitioners from business, government, law, political science, and other fields on a year long basis to grapple with topic areas listed above. This type of seminar, though expensive and difficult to undertake, is likely to be the most fruitful in terms of practical output. If only one course is to be undertaken, I would simply suggest either this multidisciplinary model or the earlier one (Appendix 4A).

NOTES

1. Frank Marini, Albert H. Rosenthal, and Robert F. Wilcox, *Science Leadership for Tomorrow, The Role of Schools of Public Affairs and Universities in Meeting Needs of Public Science Agencies.* Report of the NASPAA Committee on Science Policy and Administration (Washington, D.C.: National Association of Schools of Public Affairs and Administration, November, 1973), p. 17.
2. Robert J. Dworak, "Maintaining Service Delivery with Reduced Property Taxes," *National Civic Review* (June 1979), pp. 301–302.
3. James March and Herbert Simon, *Organizations* (New York: John Wiley and Sons, 1958).
4. American Society for Public Administration, *Report of the Subcommittee on Training* (Washington, D.C.: ASPA Program Planning Committee, July 14, 1979), p. 5.
5. J. David Roessner, *Federal Policy and the Application of Technology to State and Local Government Problems* (Washington, D.C.: National Science Foundation, April 1977).
6. David L. Wilemon, *The Role of Industry in Urban Technology Transfer: A Comparative Profile,* Report to the National Science Foundation by the Syracuse Research Corporation (Syracuse, N.Y., November 1979).

7. Roessner, *Federal Policy and the Application of Technology,* p. 19.

8. Ibid., p. 21.

9. Ibid., p. 30.

10. See, for example, W. Henry Lambright, *Adoption and Utilization of Urban Technology: A Decisionmaking Study, Executive Summary,* Report to the National Science Foundation by the Syracuse Research Corporation (Syracuse, N.Y., September 1977), p. 42.

11. Roessner, *Federal Policy and the Application of Technology,* pp. 30–31.

12. U.S. Department of Commerce, Bureau of the Census, *Statistical Abstract—1978* (Washington, D.C.: U.S. Government Printing Office, 1978), Tables 470, 498, pp. 288, 310.

13. U.S. Department of Labor, Bureau of Labor Statistics, *Occupational Outlook Handbook,* Bulletin 1955, 1978–79 Edition (Washington, D.C.: U.S. Government Printing Office), p. 773.

14. Ibid.

15. Ibid.

16. Ibid., pp. 138–139.

17. National Association of Schools of Public Affairs and Administration, *Programs in Public Affairs and Administration,* 1978 Directory (Washington, D.C., 1978), p. iii.

18. Ibid.

19. Ibid., pp. iii–iv.

20. Liz Roman Gallese, "New England Stages Economic Comeback after Decades of Woe," *The Wall Street Journal* (November 15, 1979), p. 1.

21. Richard S. Rosenbloom, "The Real Productivity Crisis Is in Government," *Harvard Business Review* (September–October 1973), pp. 156–164.

22. Samuel I. Doctors, *Technology Transfer and Utilization by State and Local Government: The Need for More and More Effective Private Sector Involvement* (Paper presented the National Science Foundation. August 1979), p. 5.

23. J. David Roessner, "The Local Government Market as a Stimulus to Industrial Innovation," paper prepared for delivery at the Workshop on Government Demand as an Instrument to Stimulate Innovation in Industry, Dublin, Ireland, June 6–7, 1978, p. 3.

24. Ibid., p. 6.

25. Ibid., p. 22.

26. Ibid., p. 21.

27. U.S. Congress, *Government Involvement in the Innovation Process: A Contractor's Report to the Office of Technology Assessment* (Washington, D.C.: U.S. Government Printing Office, 1978), p. 56.

28. Irwin Feller, Donald C. Menzel, and Lee Ann Kozak, *Diffusion of Innovations in Municipal Governments,* Executive Summary (State College, Pa.: The Pennsylvania State University Institute for Research On Human Resources, June 1976), p. 21.

29. Ibid.

30. Burton H. Klein, "The Decision Making Problem in Development," *The Rate and Direction of Inventive Activity,* Report of the National Bureau of Economic Research (Princeton, N.J.: Princeton University Press, 1962), p. 477.

31. James R. Bright, "On Appraising the Potential Significance of Radical Technological Innovations," in *Research Development and Technological Innovation,* ed. James R. Bright (Homewood, Ill.: Richard D. Irwin, Inc., 1964), pp. 435–443.

32. James Bryan Quinn, "Top Management Guides for Research Planning," in *Research Development and Technological Change,* ed. James R. Bright (Homewood, Ill.: Richard D. Irwin, Inc., 1964), pp. 677–700.

33. Donald Schon, *Technology and Change* (New York: Delacorte Press, 1965).
34. March and Simon, *Organizations*.
35. S. Colin Gilfillan, *The Sociology of Invention* (Chicago: Follett Publishing Co., 1935); David C. McClelland, *The Achieving Society* (Princeton, N.J.: D. Van Nostrand Co., 1961); Donald Schon, *Technology and Change;* Daniel Shimshoni, "Aspects of Scientific Entrepreneurship," Ph.D. dissertation, Kennedy School of Government, Harvard University, 1966.
36. Edward B. Roberts, "Entrepreneurship and Technology," in *Factors in the Transfer of Technology,* eds. William Gruber and Donald Marquis (Cambridge, Mass.: M.I.T. Press, 1969), pp. 219–238.
37. Shimshoni, "Aspects of Scientific Entrepreneurship."
38. Schon, *Technology and Change*.
39. Lambright, *Adoption and Utilization of Urban Technology*, p. 42.
40. W. Henry Lambright, "Bureaucratic Entrepreneurs," *Networking for Science and Technology in Local Government,* Proceedings of the Second Annual Innovation Group Conference, October 1977 (Washington, D.C.: U.S. Government Printing Office, 1978), p. 20.
41. Lambright, *Adoption and Utilization of Urban Technology,* p. 42.

Appendix 4A

SYLLABUS

UNIVERSITY OF PITTSBURGH
GRADUATE SCHOOL OF BUSINESS

BA 281 Management of Technological Innovation

INSTRUCTOR: Sam Doctors   Office: 2112 Cathedral of Learning

COURSE DESCRIPTION

The objective of the course is to provide an understanding of technological innovation, technical entrepreneurship, and technology transfer
that will be useful to general management, investment analysts, entrepreneurs,
and managers of R&D activities. Emphasis is on decision-making situations
involving a high degree of technological uncertainty. The viewpoint is that
of the general manager who finds himself in a fast-moving technological
environment.

MATERIALS

Materials cover the process and critical decisions through which
scientific theory, discovery, or invention emerge, and are reduced to
practice as profitable new products, processes, or services. The role of
the research development, evaluation of research proposals and results,
and the development of research policy are explored. Patent and trade
secret problems are introduced. Some national issues of science and
public policy are introduced, including the impact of federal R&D spending
patterns on technological innovation. Some attention will be devoted to
the problems of promoting technology transfer within the operating organization. Some recent research findings will be studied to determine a
profile for potential innovators, both within the organization and among
those seeking to establish new technological enterprise. Finally some
time will be devoted to the process of technological forecasting, including
some of the new techniques initially developed for the weapons acquisition
process. A technical background is not prerequisite.

TEXT   Packet of Materials
       Simons and Strasser, Science and Technology Policies (Cambridge, Mass.:
       Ballinger Press, 1973).

RESERVE MATERIALS

James Bright, Research Development and Technological Innovation.
Donald Schon, Technology and Change.
Jacob Schmookler, Invention and Economic Growth.
Edwin Mansfield, Economics of Technological Change.
The U.S. Energy Problem (NTIS-PB-207 517).

Samuel I. Doctors, The NASA Technology Transfer Program: An
  Evaluation of the Dissemination System (on reserve).
Samuel I. Doctors, The Role of Federal Agencies in Technology
  Transfer (on reserve).
Robert A. Buckles, Ideas, Inventions, and Patents: How to Protect
  Them (on reserve).
William H. Gruber and Donald G. Marquis, eds., Factors in the
  Transfer of Technology (on reserve).
Don K. Price, The Scientific Estate (on reserve).
Paul R. Lawrence and Jay W. Lorsch, Organization and Environment
  (on reserve).
Fred Warshofsky, The 21st Century: The Control of Life (on reserve).
William J. Smith and Daniel Creamer, R & D and Small Company Growth--
  Studies in Business Economics No. 102 (on reserve).
Dean Schooler, Jr., Science, Scientists and Public Policy (on reserve).
Jewkes, Sawers and Stillerman, The Sources of Invention (on reserve).
Brooks, The Government of Science--1969 (on reserve).
J. Herbert Hollomon, et al., and Michael Grenon, Energy Research and Developmen

OUTLINE

Unit I, Process of Technological Innovation (2 sessions)

    The fundamental purpose in fostering a research and development
program is to achieve an overall improvement in technological innovation.
We must look to innovations in new techniques, processes and products
as meaningful payoff from such increased knowledge. The first learning
experiences sought will be those which can be gained from studying
the innovative process in the context of a specific radical technological
innovation: phototypesetting as it evolved in the 1945 - 1961 period.

1. Case discussion Material:

         Photon A   (Bright text, pp. 157 - 171)
         Photon B   (Bright text, pp. 203 - 228)
         Photon C   (Bright text, pp. 232 - 239)

2. Readings:

         Schon, Technology and Change, pp. 1 - 41, 139 - 171.
         Bright, Research, Development, and Technological Innovation,
           pp. 69 - 91, 435 - 443.

3. Written Assignment:

         Five-hundred word paper on relevance of the conceptual frameworks
         put forward by MacLaurin and/or Schon for Photon Management at
         the close of the B Case.

4. Questions for Discussion:

    Should the new development(s) be undertaken? What information
    is relevant to this decision and by what mechanisms should
    management obtain this information? What time dimension is
    relevant in planning for the introduction of radical technological
    innovation in the Photon context? In general? How will
    industry characteristics affect acceptance of phototypesetting?
    Of innovation in general?

5. Additional Reference Materials:

    Schmookler, Invention and Economic Growth, Chapters I, III,
        and IV.
    Lawrence and Lorsch, Organization and Environment.
    Smith and Creamer, R & D and Small-Company Growth.
    Mansfield, Economics of Technological Change.

Unit II, Corporate Policy for R & D Management (2 sessions)

    Organizational objectives in a research and development program
are appropriately based upon an understanding of both the benefits
which may be anticipated from such an R & D program and the consequences
of failing to achieve effective utilization of the newly developed
technology. The student is expected to grasp some of the problems in
translating a promising technological product to a marketable end
item, including such problems as: developing an effective production
capability; establishing, early in the development cycle, two-way information links with the marketing area; training a field service
organization; assessing the magnitude of financial resources needed;
and the need to develop a corporate strategy consistent with the
introduction of a radical technological innovation.

    Part of the learning experience sought is that of appreciating
the differences between such concepts as research, applied research,
product development, and product improvement. The student is asked to
develop criteria that would govern the total amount of a firm's
research and development budget and the distribution within the budget
selected. Finally, the student should develop a conceptual framework
for innovation which takes account of the inherent conflict between the
rational and irrational views of the innovative process.

1. Case Discussion Material:
    Photon D   (Bright text, pp. 275 - 279)
    Photon E   (Bright text, pp. 313 - 321)
    Crossfield and Zip   HBS Case No. T148R* (mimeo)

2. Readings:
    Bright, pp. 21 - 31, 403 - 414.
    Richard Rosenbloom, "Product Innovation in a Scientific Age,"
        Address to the 49th Annual American Marketing Association
        Meeting, June 14, 1966 (case packet).

3. Questions for Discussion:

    How should a firm set R & D goals? What mix of R & D is appropriate
    and what criteria should be used in selecting projects? What
    production, marketing, field support, and financial resources must
    be developed to support the introduction of a new technological
    innovation such as the Photon 200 series? The Zip?

4. Additional Reference Materials:

    Jewkes, Sawers and Stillerman, "Modern Views on Invention,"
        in The Sources of Invention, Chapter II, pp. 27 - 34.
    Bright, pp. 75 - 111.
    Smith and Creamer, R & D and Small-Company Growth.

Unit III, Securing and Defending a Technical Position Through Law
(2 sessions)

There are a variety of ways to protect technology developed
within the firm. The techniques used will depend on the type of
technology, the character of the industry, and the prevailing legal
climate. Some types of technology appear to lend themselves quite
easily to the patent form of protection while others must be protected,
if at all, through maintenance of industrial security. Even if the
patent form may be available, other considerations may lead management
to avoid the patent route. Patenting statistics do indicate that the
relative rate of patenting has declined during the last three decades and
this decline may be correlated with numerous court decisions adverse to
patent holders. Further, with over two-thirds of all R & D federally
sponsored, the incentive to patent technology developed, partially or
wholly, under this federal funding is minimal given the characteristics
of the federal government market.

---

*Where materials do carry a reference to Bright text, they may be
found in the case packet.

This unit will focus primarily on the patent device as a form of legal protection for newly developed technology designed for the commercial market. Some consideration will also be devoted to the use and enforcement of a trade secret position, and to the different legal framework for the protection of intellectual property that obtains in the government contract market.

1. Case Discussion Material:

   Tansel v. Higonnet   HBS Case No. T147R (mimeo)
   Judge Caffrey   HBS Case No. T149 (mimeo)
   Wohlgemuth v. B. F. Good-
     rich, 137 Ohio Court of
     Appeals 804 (1963)   HBS Case No. T161 (mimeo)

   A Primer on Patent, Trademark, and Know-How Licensing, McNamee, Bernard J. (mimeo)
   Patent Problem: Who owns the rights?, HBR, Eaton, William W. (mimeo)

2. Reading:

   Notes on Patents   HBS Note T151R
   Defense of Inventions   HBS Note T152
   Michael Barram, "What Price Loyalty?" HBR (November-December 1968)
   Other materials will be provided.

3. Questions for Discussion:

   What strategic considerations should lead management to seek a patent position? Which considerations militate against seeking patent protection? How does the problem change when the firm is a federal contractor? What types of protection are provided by maintaining a trade secret position? What characteristics of the space/defense market discourage an active patent strategy?

4. Additional Reference Materials:

   Harris, "The Law of Trade Secrets," Lecture at George Washington University, National Law Center (1967).
   Mossinghoff and Allnutt, "Patent Infringements in Government Procurement," 42 Notre Dame Law Review (1966).
   Preston, "Patent Rights Under Federal R & D Contracts," HBR (September-October 1964).
   Welles and Waterman, "Space Technology: Payoff from Spinoff," HBR (July-August 1964).
   Scherer, et. al., Patents and the Corporation: A Report on Industrial Technology Under Public Policy.
   Buckles, Ideas, Inventions and Patents: How to Protect Them, Government Contracts Monograph No. 10, Patents and Technical Data.

Unit IV, Federal Science Policy and Industrial Innovation (2 sessions)

Since the federal government supports over two-thirds of all R & D, the patterns of this support tend to effect industrial innovation. Exact measures of these effects do not exist, yet such areas as relative U.S. foreign trade advantage, the growth rates of corporations actively engaged in areas of research largely supported by federal funds and the Boston Route 128 phenomenon are indicative of the importance in planning his R & D program or in evaluating new product areas of past, present and future federal R & D funding patterns.

The government also stimulates civilian technological development in many ways besides direct subsidies, such as: the support of basic and academic research; its policy for indexing, evaluating, and diffusing technical information; technical personnel mobility encouraged by federal policy; and the demand for novel and high performance products and services.

1. Discussion Material:

    Simons and Strasser, Science and Technology Policies (to be
        assigned).
    National Academy of Engineering, Technology Transfer and Utilization:
        Recommendations for Redirecting the Emphasis and Correcting the
        Imbalance (mimeo).
    Doctors and Akel, "Federal R & D Spending and Its Effects on
        Industrial Productivity" (mimeo).
    U.S. Department of Commerce, Technological Innovation: Its
        Environment and Management (January 1967, commonly known as
        the Charpie Report) (on reserve).

2. Questions for Discussion:

    In what ways do the patterns of federal R & D funding affect civilian
    technology? How should the manager integrate past, present, and
    future federal R & D support into his new product planning? In what
    other ways than through direct subsidization does the federal govern-
    ment stimulate civic technology?

3. Additional Reference Material:

    Rosenbloom, Technology Transfer--Process and Policy, National
        Planning Association Special Report No. 62 (1965).
    Solo, "Gearing Military R & D to Economic Growth," HBR (November-
        December 1962).
    Brooks, The Government of Science (1969).
    Price, The Scientific Estate (1965).
    Yarmolinsky, The Military Establishment: Its Impacts on
        American Society.
    Doctors, The NASA Technology Transfer Program: An Evaluation
        of the Dissemination System.
    Schooler, Science, Scientists, and Public Policy.

Unit V, Technical Entrepreneurship and the R & D Laboratory (2 sessions)

The objective of several recent research programs at M.I.T., Northwestern, and Berkeley has been to establish a more empirical model for the management of R & D. Of particular interest has been the extensive studies of Route 128 spin-off companies conducted at the M.I.T. Research Program on the Management of Science and Technology. These studies include an evaluation of the characteristics of the entrepreneurs founding these Route 128 companies; the characteristics of the technology utilized by these companies; the types of financial support needed; technical and scientific information transfer within their R & D laboratories; determinants of their success; and environmental factors contributing to the Route 128 Phenomenon.

It is important that R & D managers and researchers on the R & D management process establish a more effective dialogue. This unit seeks to provide some of the elements for such a dialogue among the participants, many of whom will soon become managers of R & D programs.

1. Discussion Material:

   Russell Peterson, "New Venture Management in a Large Company," HBR (May-June 1967).
   Edward Roberts, "Entrepreneurship and Technology,"Working Paper for the M.I.T. Research Program on the Management of Science and Technology (1967).

   Other materials will be assigned.

2. Discussion Questions:

   What is the role of entrepreneur in technology transfer? What has characterized the initiation of the Route 128 spin-off companies? Can the research results discussed in the various articles be used to enhance the R & D manager's effectiveness? How? What environmental factors help to account for the Route 128 spin-off phenomenon? Will this phenomenon continue in the Boston area? Are there other areas of the country where one could predict similar growth of technological enterprise?

3. Additional Reference Material:

   Doctors, Chapters III and IV.
   Myers, "Industrial Innovations: The Characteristics and Their Scientific and Technical Information Bases,"National Planning Association, April 1966.
   Rate and Direction of Inventive Activity, National Bureau of Economic Research (1962).
   Smith and Creamer, Science, Scientists and Public Policy.

Unit VI, Resistance to Innovation and Marketing the New Technical
Product (2 sessions)

This unit will focus on the institutional climate as it stimulates
or inhibits innovation. The operating manager must be sensitive to
environmental, institutional, political, economic, and social factors that
inhibit the acceptance of innovations. He should become aware of the
need to allocate resources to minimize the length of the market learning
curve.

The student will be expected to draw up resistance profiles for
each of the innovations introduced in the case materials. These profiles
should include such factors as: existing system, the possible elimina-
tion of job categories or skill requirements, potential conflicts with
existing laws, codes or regulations, rigidities inherent in large
bureaucratic organizations, tendency of interest groups to force conformity, and the general reluctance of an individual or group to disturb
the existing equilibrium.

1. Case Discussion Material:

Riverlake Conveyor Belt   Bright text
Sarepta Paper Company (C)   HBS Case No. T157

2. Readings:

Schon, pp. 42 - 74
Bright, pp. 130 - 135

3. Discussion Questions:

What social, economic, political and technological factors inhibited
or encouraged adoption of the given innovators? How did resistance
materialize? How does industry structure affect adoption?

4. Written Requirement:

Describe in one-or two-page paper the unique problems of marketing
new technical products. Draw up resistance profiles for each of
the innovations described in the case materials.

Unit VII, Characteristics of the Innovator (1 session)

The purpose of this unit is to acquaint students with some research
results that are important to an understanding of the successful innovator. The unit should also create a sensitivity for discerning
personality traits that are important for championing radical innovation within an existing organization or in initiating a new enterprise.
Recent research projects at Arthur D. Little, Inc., the M.I.T. Research
Program on the Management of Science and Technology, and at the Harvard
Business School (and others) may allow predictive models of successful
innovators to be constructed.

Large organizations have a special problem in the early identification of successful innovation and adopting the organization to accommodate the often independent and irascible individuals destined to champion an innovation successfully (e.g., Marconi, Rickover). The future manager must learn how to create an environment conducive to the innovator and to innovation and yet not destructive of overall organizational efficiency. The student will be encouraged to speculate about new organizational forms within the existing large organization that might create an environment conducive to change. The ethic of change is becoming an increasingly important element in promoting rapid corporate growth and yet many organizations continue to have difficulty in adapting their structure to accept and encourage change.

1. Discussion Material:

Bright, pp. 100 - 115
Schon, pp. 112 - 138
Harry Schrage, "The R & D Entrepreneur: Profile of Success,"
    HBR (November-December 1965)
Edward Roberts and Herbert Wainer, "Some Characteristics of
    Technical Entrepreneurs," a paper prepared for the M.I.T.
    Program on the Management of Science and Technology (May
    1966)

2. Discussion Questions:

Describe personality traits that appear to characterize the successful innovator. Are there any educational, social class or family characteristics that appear to be important? What characteristics would you use in constructing a predictive model of the successful innovator? How should the large organization be structured to internalize continuing change, technical and environmental? What steps should the manager take to enhance organizational adaption to change?

Unit VIII, Technological Forecasting and Assessment (2 sessions)

This final unit will examine recent advances in the art of technological forecasting. Much of the recent research in this area was presented at a conference held at Lake Placid in May 1967. The results are presented in a recent book edited by James Bright, and it is selections from this book that will form the basis for much of the discussion in this unit.

Whether it is possible to project accurately and consistently areas of radical technological innovation has not yet been established. Much experimentation with new techniques are being conducted particularly in the weapons systems area. Several of these projection techniques will be examined and the student will be asked to decide for himself the extent that technological forecasting is today a useful management decision tool.

1. Readings:

    Bright, pp. 727 - 736
    Articles to be selected from James Bright, ed., Technological
        Forecasting for Industry and Government (1968).
    Other materials will be assigned.

The Current Status of Training in Public Management of Innovations

An assessment of current training in public management of innovations or related fields is approached from three standpoints: graduate level and inservice academic training, public interest group-sponsored training, and federal government-sponsored training. With respect to the first of these categories, two principal sources will be used: a survey conducted by Cornell University in 1976 on teaching and research related to "Science, Technology and Society" (Note I), and a survey conducted by Worcester Polytechnic Institute in 1975 on methods and materials for teaching the management of technology, innovation, research and development (Note II). Two points must be made at the outset concerning both of these studies. First, both contain information on schools of public administration, business administration, law, and engineering cross-cut by the subject matter in question. Second, they are not as recent as would be desirable. However, it appears that neither has been updated since issuance.[1]

Academic Training

An analysis of the 1978 Directory of Programs in Public Affairs and Administration (PA/A) shows most clearly the emergence of separate schools of public administration. There is an increasing emphasis on public administration per se courses and a consequent lessening of integration with business or law schools. Core public administration courses generally include organization behavior and theory, statistics, general administration or management, and data processing or some kind of quantitative methods courses. In most cases, four or more courses from business administration, economics, law, and engineering can be applied toward the PA/A degree. Of the 156 graduate institutions reporting, only fourteen reported formal administrative linkages with a school of business administration. One reported a formal administration linkage with a department of engineering management. Most of the PA/A programs (98 out of 156) had at least one faculty member from business administration teaching in their program; 69 had at least one law school faculty member and 36 had an engineering school faculty member.[2]

In 1976, the Program on Science, Technology, and Society at Cornell University conducted a survey to ascertain the level of teaching and research activity going on in the area of science, technology, and society at U.S. colleges and universities.[3] Their survey, partially supported by the National Science Foundation, was designed to obtain detailed information on science, technology, and society courses and programs: what teaching materials were being used, how programs had been conceived and organized, and the kinds of students and faculty involved. Their survey questionnaires were mailed to chief academic officers at all colleges and universities in the United States as well as deans of all U.S. schools of law, medicine, and public health. They received and published information on almost 400 institutions and approximately 2,300 courses. Their survey showed a rapid increase in science, technology, and society teaching and research programs in the ten years preceding 1976.

An analysis of the Cornell directory yields valuable information on what is now available in this field at various colleges and universities. Generally speaking, most of the courses involving science, technology and society tend to be political science oriented and deal with the ethics of technology and science and technology's effects on society. The history of science and technology receives a good deal of attention. Environmental studies are featured in many of these programs. This is understandable since the survey was conducted in the mid-1970s, just about the time when governmental and academic institutions began to issue responses to the well-publicized "environmental crisis" of the late 1960s, signalled by the passage in 1969 of the National Environmental Policy Act. If science, technology, and society programs were again surveyed in the early 1980s, one would undoubtedly find a battery of energy conservation, energy and society, and energy law courses resulting from the perceived "energy crisis" of the late 1970s.

Of the 138 graduate public affairs/administration programs identified in NASPAA's 1976 Directory (1976 being used to make comparisons more timely with this 1976 Cornell Survey), fifteen were identified in the Cornell Science, Technology and Society Directory as offering graduate science and technology courses of some kind. The directory also listed three programs planned for future development involving new public administration schools to be established at three institutions. (See Note I for a list of these eighteen programs, institutions, and selected courses.) Thus, there are approximately eighteen identified out of a possible 156 (NASPAA 1978 Directory) schools of public affairs/administration that are offering graduate level science and technology-related courses as part of their programs. Even if several more have been established in the years 1977–1980, it would still be obvious that science and technology courses are not a typical offering in public affairs/public administration or graduate political science curricula.

In 1975 Robert Bjorklund and Mariann Jelinek of Worcester Polytechnic Institute conducted an international survey on methods and materials for teaching the management of technology, innovation, research and development.[4] They found great diversity in the content of courses as well as the departments responsible for them. Their sample included, however, only fourteen educational entities although in some cases more than one school or department at an institution responded. Based on their survey and their analysis of course outlines, they concluded that there are four major approaches being taken with regard to the teaching of technology, innovation, research and development. These are:

1. *Management Functions Emphasis.* This approach focuses on management of the innovative task as well as the management of innovative people. How can the classic managerial functions of planning, organizing, coordinating, controlling, and evaluating be adapted to the context of an innovative situation? About one-third of their respondents reported this approach. This approach emphasizes the special difficulties of managing creative people, establishing an innovative atmosphere, and of "estimating and controlling in the uncertainty of technologically volatile circumstances."[5]

2. *Innovation/Creativity Emphasis.* This approach focuses on the processes of creative thinking: encouraging idea generation, estimating uncertainty, or combining insights for synergistic effect. Bjorklund and Jelinek note that Innovation/Creativity is one of three areas emphasized by engineering schools and that topics range from the nature of innovation through creative thinking techniques to science fiction. This approach also emphasizes entrepreneurship and its role in innovation. Specific characteristics of innovators and the atmosphere of creativity are also Innovation/Creativity topics.[6]

3. *Policy Emphasis.* This approach has three aspects:

1. Company Policy: how does this project or product fit in with the policy of the company sponsoring the research, for example, what the company is, the markets within which it can be located, or ought to be located, and the company's plans for the future.
2. Federal Research Funding Policy: such funding determines what kinds of research and what amount of it shall be performed, in addition to what companies will be involved. Thus, federal policy shapes the course of technological development and affects the technological environment in which a company must compete.
3. International Policy: courses in this area focus on international patent and licensing agreements, technology transfer and the impact of new technology on developing countries.[7]

4. *Technology Emphasis.* This approach sees technology itself and techno-logical change as elements that make the managerial task different in an R&D setting. Technological forecasting and assessment are featured in this approach. Bjorklund and Jelinek found this approach to be favored by man-agement schools rather than engineering schools which assume students are sufficiently versed in technology.[8]

Bjorklund and Jelinek identified several gaps in the course coverage in their sample. They found first that "we seem to be teaching about accomplish-ing the innovation in the first place, rather than implementing it." Second, they found that "policy considerations of ultimate impact (on the consumer, for instance) go to the other extreme but also bypass considerations of imple-menting technological change in the company itself." Finally, with regard to entrepreneurship, they noted that "it seems to involve getting backing and funding for the initial development, rather than implementation of later stages, say, of making an innovation a commercial reality."[9]

In the conclusion of their report, the two authors make this important point:

> It's also a fairly safe bet that courses on the management of technology, innovation, research and development will be around for a long while to come. It has been widely suggested that the rate of change of technology is increasing at an increasing rate. This can only intensify managers' needs to deal with innovation, technology and R&D in the most effective, efficient ways—suggesting a continuing market for technolo-gy, innovation and research and development management courses.[10]

The institutions which responded and the courses they reported to the Worcester Polytechnic Institute are shown in Note II.

Business Schools

The American Association of Collegiate Schools of Business annually gathers information on schools of business which it transcribes onto school fact forms. Their recent (1978-1979) surveys do not contain any questions concerning whether a school conducts technology-related courses. There is a category, "other," where schools can list other kinds of courses about which the survey did not inquire. None of the schools reported any technology-related courses.[11]

Law Schools

The current training in law schools with respect to management of technologi-cal change or science and technology was assessed through the use of the 1979-80 *Directory of Law Teachers* and the Cornell University directory men-tioned above. The Directory of Law Teachers lists law teachers by subject ar-eas.[12] The first relevant area listed with respect to this paper is "Law and Science," an area which includes computers, technology, technology assessment, and jurimetrics. Seventy-three faculty were listed under law and science, representing a total of fifty-six law schools. When you peruse the list of courses offered, however, very few relate to public management of innovations. Note III shows a sampling of law school offerings, omitting those law and science categories obviously irrelevant to this paper such as computers and the law, law and medicine, law and statistics, and environmental law. A second relevant area is "Patents, Copyrights, Trademarks," which includes intellectual property and protection of ideas. Courses in this area are also listed in Note III.

A Representative University Inservice Program

Many universities offer special courses or professional development summer institutes for executives and managers who wish to expand their knowledge and/or improve their skills. These can range from five-week intensive summer sessions for which the university accepts a limited number of applicants to varied course offerings of one- to five-day seminars which any interested person can attend upon payment of a registration fee.

The Division of Management Education of the University of Michigan's Graduate School of Business Administration is representative of institutions offering the latter kinds of courses. A review of their 1979–1980 *Management Seminars Catalogue* lists fifty available courses. Four of these are categorized under "Management in Public Organizations." One concerns labor negotiations, and two concern budgeting techniques. The fourth, entitled "Managing Revenue Reduction in the Public Sector," is about alternative fiscal strategies, such as trimming the budget and productivity: for example, improving work methods. Two management courses offered at Michigan come close to addressing the kinds of issues involved in public management of innovations as discussed in this chapter. One is "Confronting Realities in Product Innovation" which concerns product innovation strategy, the innovation development process and organizing for implementation. The suggested students for this seminar, however, are executives or professionals from "industries where successful product innovation is necessary for continued growth and profitability." Thus, the utility of some of the kinds of material contained in this course to public sector managers is not recognized. One other course offers one component—out of nine—which might come under the general topic of public management of innovations. Michigan's "New Frontiers of Management" course devotes one-ninth of its outline to "Managing New Technologies," specifically technology and the managerial function, and motivating the technological work force. The catalogue suggests both public and private sector managers could benefit from this material.

Public Interest Group Training

One of the public interest groups which has had a long-standing commitment to strong professional training for local government administrators is the International City Management Association (ICMA). Since 1934, ICMA has provided inservice training through courses based primarily on the Municipal Management Series texts. The ICMA's Training Institute offers individual and group correspondence courses, self-administered training programs, and workshops and seminars. The intention of the Institute is to "meet the needs of today's local government administrators." In 1978–1979, fifteen courses were offered. (See Note IV.)

A review of the ICMA courses available shows that public management of innovations is not included as part of the curricula. The "basic principles" course includes systems analysis as a topic, and the local government personnel administration course addresses the issue of productivity, but that is the extent of treatment of issues related to public management of innovations.

As the professional association which puports to represent public managers at every level of government and in every program field, the American Society for Public Administration (ASPA) believes it "has a responsibility to enhance the knowledge and skills required of its members to maintain and improve vital public services at a time of cutbacks and limits on revenues and expenditures."[13] In 1978 and 1979, an ASPA subcommittee on training studied ASPA's training policies and programs, including the feasibility of establishing an ASPA training program with appropriate staffing at the national level.

Subcommittee staff conducted a needs assessment study in May 1979 by polling ASPA chapter presidents who represent the over 16,000 members of ASPA. Sixty percent of the 101 chapter presidents responded. One question that was asked concerned other types of training provided and whether these offered training in the chapter president's geographical area. Eighty-six percent of the chapter presidents responding indicated local colleges and universities did offer training; 52 percent said other professional associations did; and 46 percent said private consultants offered training. Thirty-two percent mentioned state leagues and county associations, and 32 percent mentioned state personnel departments.[14]

Even though a myriad of existing programs were cited, 32 percent of the respondents thought these programs were not meeting chapter members' needs and 45 percent were not sure. Chapter presidents suggested ASPA should "work cooperatively with local resources such as universities and other providers in order to complement existing resources."[15]

As a result of the subcommittee's recommendations, a Public Administration Training Center was established at ASPA headquarters in the spring of 1980. Its purpose is "to enhance the professional development of public managers at the federal, state, and local levels through training and other high-priority management development programs for ASPA members and potential members." In 1980 the center's program, to include management training and career development, among other topics, was developed. The subcommittee report suggests several of these efforts might be suitable for grant or contract funding.

The subcommittee also recommended these kinds of activities for the center's first two years: pilot workshops in various cities; expansion of section workshops at the national ASPA conference; pre- or postconference workshops at each regional conference; and development of grant proposals to provide additional resources for program design, curriculum development and actual training.

Federal Training

The Office of Personnel Management (OPM) offers a variety of training programs for federal, state, and local government employees. These courses are designed for all types of employees from clerical to executive. This training is delivered through a nationwide system which included the Federal Executive Institute and four Executive Seminar Centers, as well as training centers in Washington, D.C. and in each of the ten regions. OPM's training system also includes the National Independent Study Center, the National Indian Training Center, and the Southwest Intergovernmental Training Center. There are six interagency training centers in Washington, D.C. Each covers a different curriculum area, operates on a reimbursable basis, and conducts on-site training courses on request in addition to regularly scheduled courses. Each of OPM's ten regions has a Regional Training Center which offers courses in the same curriculum areas as the six Washington centers.

The Federal Executive Institute (FEI) is a residential training facility located in Charlottesville, Virginia. FEI was established by presidential order to serve the training and development requirements of federal executives, grades GS-16 and above or the equivalent. The institute's curriculum stresses these three broad areas: the environment of federal executive performance, management systems and processes, and interpersonal and personal executive effectiveness.

OPM also operates four residential interagency Executive Seminar Centers in Berkeley, California; Kings Point, New York; Oak Ridge, Tennessee; and Wilmington, Delaware. Nine different two-week seminars are offered by each center. The purposes of these seminars are to develop and broaden the skills and knowledge of new and advancing managers in public policy, public programs, the national economy, science and technology, the environment and natural resources, intergovernmental relations, and other areas.[16]

OPM provides correspondence courses through the National Independent Study Center in Denver, Colorado. These courses offer self-contained course materials in the areas of personnel management, labor relations, equal employment opportunity, and communications and office skills.

The Southwest Intergovernmental Training Center in San Antonio, Texas was established under the Sixteen-Point Program for the Spanish Speaking. It offers forty-three academic and technical skills training courses primarily for those in grades GS-7 and below. There is also a Federal Acquisition Institute in Alexandria, Virginia designed to develop the skills and knowledge of federal employees engaged in procurement, production, systems acquisition, and grants management.

OPM has a National Training Curriculum which is offered by the six interagency training centers in Washington, D.C. mentioned above, as well as all of OPM's ten regional training centers. Four of the six subject areas offered are automatic data processing, communications and office skills, labor relations, and personnel management. The two others which are more germane to the subject of this paper are general management and management sciences.

An analysis of OPM's 1979–1981 *Catalog of Interagency Training Courses* which includes the courses offered at all of the facilities discussed above as well as a limited number of courses designed specifically for employees of particular mission agencies, reveals no courses specifically geared to the public management of innovations as defined in this chapter. There are, however, numerous courses available under the auspices of various OPM facilities which offer subject matter closely related, or easily adaptable, to public management of innovations curricula.

In the general management area, there are approximately eighty-four courses in these four categories: government affairs, legal education institute, management training, and supervisory and intern courses. The courses range from the fundamental to the advanced and specialized. A list of the pertinent general management courses can be found in Note V. Of these, the one which could most easily be modified to include a public management of innovations component is the Executive Seminar Center program on Science, Technology and Public Policy. Other more general management courses listed in Note V, however, could be adapted. Of the eighty-eight courses in management sciences offered by OPM, only two appear relevant to this chapter. These two, shown in Note VI, focus more on the contracting/procurement/R&D management functions.

NOTES

1. A telephone call to Cornell University in November 1979 produced the information that their report had not been updated and no plans were under way to do so. A telephone call to Worcester Polytechnic Institute revealed that both professors who conducted the survey were no longer at the institute and that their whereabouts were unknown.

2. National Association of Schools of Public Affairs and Administration, *Programs in Public Affairs and Administration*, 1978 Directory (Washington, D.C., 1978).

3. Cornell University Programs on Science, Technology and Society, *Science, Technology and Society: A Guide to the Field, Directory of Teaching, Research and Resources in the U.S.*, compiled and edited by Ezra D. Heitowit, Jane Epstein, and Gerald M. Steinberg (Ithaca, N.Y., 1976).

4. Robert Bjorklund and Mariann Jelinek, "Teaching Technology: A Review of Approaches and Materials," Preliminary Report, Department of Managing Engineering, Worcester Polytechnic Institute (Worcester, Mass., November 14, 1975).

5. Ibid., p. 3.

6. Ibid., pp.3–4.

7. Ibid., p. 5.

8. Ibid., pp. 5–6.

9. Ibid., p. 9.

10. Ibid., p. 10.

11. Telephone conversation with Audrey Easton, American Association of Collegiate Schools of Business, November 20, 1979.

12. Association of American Law Schools, *Directory of Law Teachers*, 1979–1980 Edition (St. Paul, Minn.: West Publishing Co., 1979).
13. American Society for Public Administration, *Report of the Subcommittee on Training* (Washington, D.C.: Program Planning Committee, July 14, 1979), p. 1.
14. Ibid., p. 6.
15. Ibid., p. 7.
16. Office of Personnel Management, *Interagency Training, 1979–81 Catalog of Courses, Washington, D.C. Metropolitan Area* (Washington, D.C.: U.S. Government Printing Office, 1979), p. 284.

NOTE I
Cornell University Survey of Graduate Programs with Science, Technology, and Society Courses

I.   San Jose University
     Offers Master's Degree in Cybernetic Systems through its School of Social Science. In 1976, they planned to develop closer cooperation with the Graduate School of Urban Planning and Public Administration.
          Cybernetic Systems courses: Evolution of Technical Innovation
                                      Technology Assessment
                                      Technology Transfer (geared to developing nations)
                                      Telecommunications

II. University of Southern California
     Eng.: Technology and Society
     Planning and Urban Studies: Public Policy and the Urban Environment
     Pub. Adm.: Science, Technology, and Government

III. University of Denver
     Technology, Modernization, and International Studies (TMIS) Program of the Graduate School of International Studies.
     TMIS: Technology and Modernization
           Management and Planning of Technology
           Analytical Methods for Technological Decisionmakers
           Technological Processes

IV. American University
     Science/Technology Policy and Administration—(STPA) Program under the College of Public Affairs
     STPA: Change and the Managerial Process
           Technological Forecasting and Assessment
           Politics and Economics of Research and Development
           Planning and Control of R & D Operations
           Gov't and Public Admin.: Science, Technology and Government
                                    Public Management of Science

V. George Washington University
   Graduate Program in Science, Technology, and Public Policy (STPP)
   under the School of Public and International Affairs.
   Pol. Sci.: Science, Technology, and Public Affairs
           Government, Science, and Technology
   Bus. Adm.: Technological Change and Manpower
           Seminar: Science, Technology and Public Policy

VI. Indiana University
   Advanced Studies in Science, Technology, and Public Policy. Independent with principal courses cross-listed with the Department of Political Science and the School of Public and Environmental Affairs (PEA).
   PEA: Technology Assessment
        Urban Technology

VII. Purdue University
   Program on Science, Technology, and Public Policy (STPP) under the Department of Political Science. In 1976, planning a complementary program in Public Policy and Public Administration.
   Pol. Sci.: Science and Government
          American Public Policies
          (decisionmaking in technologically complex policy arenas)
          Science, Technology, and Public Policy
          Science and the City

VIII. University of Minnesota
   In 1976, a joint graduate degree program between Engineering and Public Affairs was planned.
   Eng.: Engineering for New Priorities
   Pub. Aff.: Technology Planning
   Soc. Sci.: Ecology, Technology, and Society

IX. Princeton University
   Center for Environmental Studies (CES) was in 1976 planning a Technology and Public Policy graduate program.
   Pol. Sci.: Science, Technology, and Politics
          Technology and International Relations
   Pub. and Int'l Aff.: Ecological Theory and Public Policy
   Eng. and App. Sci.: Introduction to Technological Challenges

X. University of New Mexico
   Program for Advanced Study in Public Science Policy and Administration (PA)
   Pub. Adm.: Seminar: Public Science Policy and Administration

XI. Cornell University
   Program on Policies for Science and Technology In Developing Nations (PPSTDN).
   Program on Science, Technology and Society (STS)
   Bus. and Pub. Adm.: Science, Technology, and Development
               Science, Technology, and Public Policy in the U.S.
               Science, Technology and International Relations

The Politics of Technical Decisions
The Impact and Control of Technological Change
Law: Legal and Market Controls of Technological Change Seminar
on Science, Technology, and Law
XII. Syracuse University.
Engineering and Public Affairs (EPA) within the College of Engineering Program on Technology and Society (PTS).
PTS/Natural and App. Sci.: Social Aspects of Technology
Science, Technology, and Public Policy
Pol. Sci.: Political Dynamics of Large-Scale Technological Programs
Pub. Adm.: Post-Industrial Administration
The City and Technological Change
XIII. University of Oklahoma
Science and Public Policy Program (SPPP).
Pol. Sci.: Science, Technology and Public Policy
Science, Technology, and International Politics
XIV. Carnegie-Mellon University
Engineering and Public Affairs (EPA) joint with the School of Urban and Public Affairs.
EPA: Systems Analysis and Urban Problems
Law and the Engineer
Law and Technology
Products Liability
Emerging Problems in Technology
Engineering and Public Affairs: Special Topics
Civ. Eng.: Urban Engineering Issues and Problems
XV. Lehigh University
Graduate Program in Public Administration with concentration on Science, Technology, and Public Policy.
Int'l Rel.: Science, Technology, and International Relations
International Law and Technological Change
Soc. Rel: Science, Technology, and Society
XVI. Pennsylvania State University
Science, Technology, and Society Program (STS).
STS/Eng.: Technology: Its Character, Role, and Function
STS: Technological Change: Its Production, Diffusion, and Impact
Science and Public Policy
XVII. University of Pittsburgh
Bus. Adm.: Management of Technological Change
Indust. Eng.: Technology Systems Management
XVIII. University of Washington
Program in Social Management of Technology (SMT).
SMT: Technology Assessment
Technology, Society, and Public Policy
Urban Technology and Urban Policy
Pub. Adm.: Seminar in Science and Public Policy
International Science and Technology Policy

NOTE II
Worcester Polytechnic Institute Survey of Technology, Innovation, Research and Development Courses

I. Engineering Departments
   Clarkson College Department of Management
     Course Title: Management of Technology
   Northwestern University Department of Industrial Engineering and Management Science:
     Organization of R & D
   University of Pittsburgh School of Engineering
     Technology Management Seminar
     Management of Innovation
   University of Trondeim, Norwegian Institute of Technology
     Management of Innovation and Creativity
   Vanderbilt University School of Engineering
     Management of Technology
II. Management or Business Schools
   Delaware Business Administration Department
     BU 447
   George Washington University School of Government and Business Administration
     International Science and Technology
     Technological Change and Manpower
     Administration of R & D
   Innovation Management Institute (Canada)
     Supervision and Management of R & D Personnel
   Manchester University Business School
     Management of R & D
   Oregon—College of Business Administration
     Technological Organizations
     Technology and Innovation
   Pennsylvania—Wharton School, Department of Management
     Technology and Corporate Structure
   University of Pittsburgh Graduate School of Business
     Management of Technological Innovation
III. Public Administration
   American University—School of Public Affairs
     Management of R & D

NOTE III
Law Schools Offering Science/Technology Courses*

Law School	Course(s)
American University	Law and Science
Arizona State University	Law and Science
Arizona, University of	Law and Science
Arkansas, University of—Fayetteville	Law and Technology
Bridgeport, University of	Law and Science
California Western	Law and Technology
Cincinnati, University of	Law and Science
Columbia	Law and Science
Connecticut, University of	Law and Technology
Cornell	Law and Science
Denver, University of	Law and Science
Detroit College of Law	Law and Science
Franklin-Pierce	Law and Science
Georgetown	Law and Science
George Washington	Atomic Energy
	Law and Science
	Legal Problems of Technological Hazards
Harvard	International Response to Science and Technology
Illinois Institute of Technology Chicago-Kent College of Law	Law and Technology
Indiana University	Law and Technology
	Legal Process and Technological Change
Iowa, University of	Law and Science
John Marshall	Law and Science
Kansas, University of	Law and Science
Louisville, University of	Law and Science
Maryland, University of	Law and Science
Memphis State	Atomic Energy
	Law, Science and Technology
Michigan, University of	Law and Science
Northwestern	Law and Science

*Note that this list omits those law and science categories irrelevant to this chapter such as computers and law, law and medicine, law and statistics, and environmental law.

Source: Association of American Law Schools. *Directory of Law Teachers*, 1979–80 edition (St. Paul, Minn.: West Publishing Co., 1979).

Notre Dame	Law and Technology
Ohio State	Law and Science
Pennsylvania, University of	Atomic Energy
	Law and the Energy Crisis
	Law and Science
Puget Sound	Control of Technology
Southern California, University of	Law and Science
Southern Methodist	Law and Science
Temple	Law and Science
Tennessee, University of	Law and Science
Tulsa, University of	Law, Science and Technology
Vanderbilt	Law and Science
Virginia, University of	Law and Science
Washington University (St. Louis)	Law and Science
Yeshiva	Law and Science
	Technology, Personhood and Risk

Law Schools Offering Courses in Patents, Copyrights, Trademarks (Including Intellectual Property and Protection of Ideas)*

Law School	Course(s)
Alabama, University of	Patents, Copyrights, Trademarks
Albany Law School, Union University	Patents, Copyrights, Trademarks
American	Copyright
Arizona, University	Patent and Copyright Law
	Patents, Copyrights, Trademarks
Baltimore University of	Patents, Copyrights, Trademarks
Baylor	Patents, Copyrights, Trademarks
Boston College	Copyright
Boston University	Patents, Copyrights, Trademarks
California, University of—Berkeley	Patents, Copyrights, Trademarks
California, University of—L.A.	Advanced Copyright Law
	Copyright Law
	Copyrights, Trademarks
	Freedom of Speech
Capital	Patents, Copyrights
	Patents, Copyrights, Trademarks
Chicago, University of	Patents, Copyrights, Trademarks
Cleveland-Marshall	Patents, Copyrights, Trademarks
Colorado, University of	Patents, Copyrights, Trademarks

Source: Association of American Law Schools. *Directory of Law Teachers,* 1979–80 edition (St. Paul, Minn.: West Publishing Co., 1979).

Columbia	Patents, Copyrights, Trademarks
Connecticut, University of	Copyright
Dalhousie	Patents, Copyrights, Trademarks
Denver, University of	Patents, Copyrights, Trademarks
Detroit	Copyright Law
	Intellectual Property
	Patents, Copyrights, Trademarks
Duke	Patents, Copyrights, Trademarks (Entertainment Law; Intellectual Property)
	Patents, Copyrights, Trademarks (Motion Picture Production, Finance, Distribution)
Emory	Copyright and Unfair Competition
	Patents, Copyrights, Trademarks
Florida State	Patents, Copyrights, Trademarks
Franklin-Pierce	Law/Science Interfaces
	Patent Litigation
	Patents, Copyrights, Trademarks
George Washington	Patents, Copyrights, Trademarks
Georgetown	Copyright
Georgia, University of	Patents and Copyrights
Golden Gate	Copyright
Gonzaga	Patents, Copyrights, Trademarks (Environmental Law)
Harvard	Patents, Copyrights, Trademarks
Hawaii, University of	Intellectual Property
Hofstra	Copyright
Houston, University of	Intellectual Property
	Patents, Copyrights, Trademarks
Howard	Patents, Copyrights, Trademarks
Illinois, University of	Patent Law
Indiana	Patents and Antitrusts
John Marshall	Patents, Copyrights, Trademarks
Kansas, University of	Patents, Copyrights, Trademarks
Louisville, University of	Patent Law
Loyola (Loyola-Marymount)	Intellectual Property
Loyola (New Orleans)	Patents
	Patents, Copyrights, Trademarks
McGeorge (University of the Pacific)	Patents, Copyrights, Trademarks
Marquette	Patents, Copyrights, Trademarks
Maryland, University of	Patents, Copyrights, Trademarks
Memphis State	Copyrights
Miami, University of	Patents, Copyrights, Trademarks
Michigan, University of	Copyrights
Minnesota, University of	Patents, Copyrights, Trademarks
Missouri-Columbus, University of	Patents, Copyrights, Trademarks
Montana	Patents, Copyrights

Nebraska, University of	Copyrights
	Patents, Copyrights, Trademarks
New England	Copyright Law
New York Law School	Patents, Copyrights, Trademarks
New York University	Copyright
North Carolina Central	Patents, Copyrights, Trademarks
North Carolina, University of	Patents and Copyright Law
Northeastern University	Patents, Copyrights, Trademarks
Northern Illinois	Patents, Copyrights, Trademarks
Northern Kentucky	Patents, Copyrights, Trademarks
Ohio Northern University (Pettit College of Law)	Patents, Copyrights, Trademarks
Oklahoma, University of	Patents, Copyrights, Trademarks
Oregon, University of	Patents, Copyrights, Trademarks
Pennsylvania, University of	Copyrights
	Patents, Copyrights, Trademarks
Puget Sound	Patents, Copyrights, Trademarks
Rutgers, Newark	Patents, Copyrights, Trademarks
St. Louis	Copyright and Law
San Diego, University of	Patents, Copyrights, Trademarks
San Francisco, University of	Patents, Copyrights, Trademarks
Santa Clara, University of	Patents, Copyrights, Trademarks
Seton Hall	Intellectual Property
South Carolina	Patents, Copyrights, Trademarks
South Dakota	Patents, Copyrights, Trademarks
Stanford	Copyright, Patents, Trademarks, and Related State Doctrines
State University of N.Y. at Buffalo	Patents, Copyrights, Trademarks
Suffolk	Patents, Copyrights, Trademarks
Syracuse	Copyright
	Patents, Copyrights, Trademarks
Tennessee	Patents, Copyrights, Trademarks
Texas Southern	Patents and Copyrights
Texas Tech	Patents, Copyrights, Trademarks
Texas, University of	Patents, Copyrights, Trademarks
Tulane	Patents, Copyrights, Trademarks
Utah, University of	Patents, Copyrights, Trademarks
Villanova	Trademarks, Copyrights, and Unfair Competition
Virginia, University of	Patents, Copyrights, Trademarks
Washington and Lee	Intellectual Property
	Patents, Copyrights, Trademarks (Trademarks and Unfair Trade Practices)
Washington University (St. Louis)	Patents, Trademarks, Copyrights
Wayne State	Patents, Copyrights, Trademarks
Western New England College	Patents, Copyrights, Trademarks

William and Mary	Patents, Copyrights, Trademarks
Wisconsin	Patents, Copyrights, Trademarks
Yale	Patents, Copyrights, Trademarks
Yeshiva	Patents, Copyrights, Trademarks

NOTE IV
ICMA Training Institute: 1978–1979 Courses*

1. Managing the Modern City
2. Local Government Personnel Administration
3. Effective Supervisory Practices
4. Local Government Police Management
5. Managing Fire Services
6. Management Policies in Local Government Finance
7. Principles and Practice of Urban Planning
8. Managing Human Services
9. Public Relations in Local Government
10. Urban Public Works Administration
11. Managing Municipal Leisure Services
12. Policy Analysis in Local Government
13. Small Cities Management Training
14. Personnel Evaluation in Local Government
15. Women in Local Government Management

NOTE V
U.S. Government Office of Personnel Management General Management Courses

I. Federal Executive Institute
   A. Executive Leadership and Management Program
      Three-week course
      Executives recently promoted to GS-16 or above only
      Relevant content: Skills and knowledge of most crucial concern to individuals in transition to federal executive ranks.
   B. Senior Executive Education Program
      Seven-week course
      Career and noncareer senior executives
      Relevant content: Participants construct an individual learning program, e.g., self-assessment, organizational behavior, national needs and priorities, management systems and processes.

*Source: ICMA Training Institute, *1978–79 Catalogue of Courses.*

II. Executive Seminar Centers
    A. Administration of Public Policy
        Two-week course
        Federal GS 13–15 and equivalent for state and local employees
        Relevant content: Interaction and effects of change on our technology, our social systems, and our political structures. Study of the move from unilateral federal administration of programs toward delivery of public services through shared responsibilities with state and local governments.
    B. Domestic Policies and Programs
        Two-week course
        Federal GS 13–15 and equivalent for state and local employees
        Relevant content: domestic policy making and program implementation processes—urban and suburban challenges
    C. Public Program Management
        Two-week course
        Federal GS 13–15 and equivalent for state and local employees
        Relevant content: Public expectation of bureaucratic responsiveness; improving delivery systems; new challenges facing program managers because of social, political and technological changes; program manager as an agent of positive change.
    D. Science, Technology and Public Policy
        Two-week course
        Federal GS-13–15 and equivalent for state and local employees
        Relevant content: Review the nature of science and technology as it exists in government agencies; organization and management of various science programs; capacity and responsiveness of government and nongovernment institutions that deal with science and technology; transfer of technological innovations between the public and private sectors; development of the capacity for technological assessment.
    E. Seminar for Advancing Managers
        Two-week course
        Experienced managers with some previous formal management training
        Relevant content: Working effectively within the several environments of government management; productivity improvement approaches; implementing and evaluating programs.

III. Office of Personnel Management
    A. Education for Public Management
        Full Academic Year Program held at Cornell, Harvard, Indiana University, Massachusetts Institute of Technology, Princeton, University of Southern California, University of Virginia, and University of Washington
        Federal GS 12–14 and equivalent for state and local employees
        Relevant content: Further training of selected midcareerists; mix of management subjects; subjects related to agency mission and various personal electives.

B. Management Institute for Scientists and Engineers
Five-day program; offered three times a year
First-line supervisors of working technical groups or scientists/engineers about to assume supervisory responsibility (usually GS 11–15 or equivalent)
Relevant content: Special nature of the managerial job in R & D and in other engineering and scientific organizations; leadership patterns to accelerate creativity, administrative practices which permit the most effective direction and control of technical projects. Staff drawn from government, leading industrial organizations, and universities.
C. Management of Scientists and Engineering Organizations—An Executive Institute
Five-day program; offered twice a year; thirty scientists/engineers (GS-15 and above) who have management responsibility for science and engineering programs.
Relevant content: Management planning for R & D; operational environment of scientists and engineers in government; comparison of R & D management in other areas.

NOTE VI
U.S. Government Office of Personnel
Management Management Sciences Courses

I. Office of Personnel Management
A. Contracting with Small Business Enterprises
Two-day course
Open to contract specialists, contract administrators, contracting officers, and others whose job duties interface with the foregoing categories.
Relevant content: Develops participants' sensitivity to the problems faced by small businesses and improves the ability of procurement personnel to deal with small businesses.
B. Research and Development Contracting
Five-day course
Open to program managers of research and development projects, contract and procurement specialists, contract administrators, project engineers, and those whose job duties interface with the foregoing categories.
Relevant content: Entire cycle of R & D procurement from initiation of the requirement to completion of the project.

Index

Samuel I. Doctors is Professor of Business Administration at the Graduate School of Business, University of Pittsburgh, and Director of the Energy Policy Institute at the university. Professor Doctors is a consultant to the Intergovernmental Science and Research Program, the National Science Foundation, the Federal Emergency Management Agency, and the Department of Energy. He was formerly Associate Director and Consultant to the President's Advisory Council on Minority Business Enterprise for the National Strategy and Goals, as well as consultant to the Office of Economic Opportunity and various private firms in management education and fair employment practices. Professor Doctors is the author or coauthor of seven books, including *The Role of Federal Agencies in Technology Transfer, The Management of Technological Change,* and most recently *Individual Energy Conservation Behaviors* (Oelgeschlager, Gunn & Hain, 1980). In addition to these and other books, he has authored numerous articles and reports on consumerism, management and technical assistance for minority enterprise, small business, energy, technology transfer, and the management of technological innovations. He is currently involved in an evaluation of the Urban Technology Transfer System and a study on small business energy usage.

W. Henry Lambright is Professor of Political Science and Public Administration at the Maxwell School, Syracuse University, and Director of the Science and Technology Policy Center at Syracuse Research Corporation. Professor Lambright is a specialist in government as it relates to science, technology, innovation, and organizational change. He is the author of *Governing Science and Technology; Technology Transfer to Cities: Processes of Choice at the Local Level;* and numerous articles, monographs, reports, and professional papers. In the past, he has held the positions of special assistant with the National Aeronautics and Space Administration and guest scholar at the Brookings Institution. Professor Lambright has also served as a consultant to numerous federal and state agencies.

Donald C. Stone is well known in the field of public administration both in the public and academic settings. He has served the government in various capacities, including Assistant Director of the Bureau of the Budget, Executive Office of the President; member of U.S. delegations and representative of the State Department in establishing the United Nations system; and Director of Administration of the Marshall Plan and other assistance programs. He has served as consultant to nearly one hundred state and local governments as well as eighteen federal agencies and twenty-four foreign countries. In addition, Professor Stone has held faculty appointments at several universities. He was President of Springfield College and Dean of the University of Pittsburgh's Graduate School of Public and International Affairs. Currently, he holds the position of Adjunct Professor of Public Administration at the School of Urban and Public Affairs, Carnegie-Mellon University. At the same time, he is Chairman of the International Association of Schools and Institutes of Administration and serves on the Executive Committee of the American Consortium for International Public Administration. Professor Stone is author of several books, numerous reports, and about three hundred articles.